WARRIORS IN TRANSITION

A Memoir in Twenty-Eight Stories

by Ellen Woods

Copyright © 2014 by Ellen Woods

All rights reserved. No part of this publication may be reproduced or transmitted in any form or by any means, electronic or mechanical, including photocopy, recording, or any information storage and retrieval system, without permission in writing from the publisher

Published in the United States by the Word Project Press of Sonora, CA

Requests for permission to make copies of any part of this work should be submitted online at
info@wordprojectpress.com

Credits:

Author Photo:
Liliana Titterton

Cover Art: Ellen Woods
Cover Design: Melody Baker

ISBN-13: 978-0-9890682-5-3
ISBN-10: 0989068250

*For my writing mentors
Kathleen McClung and Sue Moon
who believed I could find and express
the stories within me.*

ACKNOWLEDGEMENTS

My gratitude to the editors of the literary magazines noted in *Published Work* for publishing individual stories before they came together as this book.

Many thanks to Gillian P. Herbert of Word Project Press for her enthusiastic support and encouragement to make *Warriors in Transition* happen. And special thanks to Victoria Zackheim for her editorial expertise in refining these stories, her trust in my vision, and her extraordinary kindness.

I honor my late parents, Nancy and Winton Woods Sr., for inspiring this book.

My deepest gratitude to my daughter Liliana for the layout and final editing of *Warriors in Transition*. Her close reading, sensitive perceptions and constructive suggestions were crucial to the completion of this project.

I am grateful to Shizue Seigel for her skillful and generous collaboration on the front cover design.

I have been encouraged and stimulated by writing groups: the Spasso Writing Group, The Reverie Writing Group, the SF Aquatic Park Writing Group, the Montclair Women's Writing Group, and the Memoir Continuation Group.

And to my family and my trusted friends; my spiritual teachers Maylie Scott, Sojun Mel Weitzman, and Rev Dr. Joan Steadman; and the guardians of my psyche, Sally DeWees, Ann Smith, and Margaret Skinner, I could not have done this without you.

TO THE READER

Many of the people in these stories have been given a pseudonym, and distinguishing details have been changed to protect privacy. I have made a good faith effort to convey the essence of what I recount, and some events have been compressed to meet the needs of the story. Dialogue is an approximation, as in all memoirs, especially in stories from the distant past.

WARRIORS IN TRANSITION

PART ONE: 1951 – 1983

1. Ruby's Grace — 1
2. Do unto Others — 7
3. Mother May I? — 13
4. Blood Sisters — 21
5. Exposure — 31
6. Got Your Back — 37
7. Courtly Love — 45
8. Gateway — 51
9. Black Power — 55
10. The Power of Sisterhood — 63

PART TWO: 1985 – 1989

11. Transforming — 71
12. Darkness — 75
13. Intuitively Speaking — 79
14. Green Bough in My Heart — 87

PART THREE: 1995-2007

15. Show of Support — 97
16. Miss Pretty — 105
17. Becoming — 113
18. Tumbleweed — 121
19. Defenseless — 127
20. The Green Dragon — 133
21. Warriors in Transition — 139

PART FOUR: 2010 – 2014

22. Wild Turkeys Rising   151
23. Pick and Pull   155
24. Dayzhavous   161
25. We Are Family   171
26. Joy of Cooking   179
27. Boomerang Babes   187
28. The Wisdom of Waiting   195

PART ONE

1951-1983

RUBY'S GRACE

Sitting on the cool, green linoleum tiles beside Barney, my family's beloved Irish Setter, I could almost disappear into his fur. He was sleeping, snoring quietly, saliva dripping onto the floor. I ran my fingers down his back and along his tail, releasing a fine layer of hair. He exhaled, almost like a sigh, and quivered. It was a lazy afternoon in Centerville, Ohio, 1951. Barney and I were both six years old.

"You gonna pull that dog's hair out, Precious, just you wait and see," said my babysitter. Ruby had a way of scolding that made me laugh. She was never mean; she just knew who I was. When she laughed, I felt happy. "I know you love that dog," she added, and she was right. Barney was my best friend, and Ruby seemed to accept the naturalness of my attachment.

I smiled shyly, comforted as always by this woman's presence. Although I hadn't known her long, she felt like family. I liked coming home from school and finding Ruby there. Two afternoons each week, she stayed with me while my mother volunteered at my older sister's Girl Scout troop. My brother was in the sixth grade and, in my mind, practically a grown-up.

Ruby had begun doing housework for us months earlier, shortly after we moved to Ohio. A shy child, I was slow to make friends. My shyness had increased the year before, at my old school, when I learned that I was a gentile, one of two students in the class who was not Jewish. No one played with us, and I felt there was a badness about me that kept them away. And now, in this new school, I was afraid it might happen again. I didn't like feeling different. I was lonely.

I watched Ruby slide the iron along the sleeve of my father's shirt, gliding back and forth like a swan on a crystal lake. She was dressed in her usual black dress with starched white apron and collar, beautifully ironed, and emitting the aroma of flowers. My mother had taught me that every woman needed to know how to iron, although I wasn't allowed to do it until I was older. I couldn't wait to try, and I hoped Mom would let Ruby teach me.

Ruby hummed as she ironed the collar one last time. "Your daddy needs a nice pressed shirt for work," she said, shaking it out and placing it on a hanger. I can still see her elegant hands buttoning the top two buttons. As she completed the task, she sang:

> *Wade in the water, wade in the water*
> *Children wade in the water*
> *God's gonna trouble the water.*
>
> *Who's that young girl dressed in red,*
> *Must be the children Moses led,*
> *And God's gonna trouble the water.*

I felt as if I were being rocked in her arms, and imagined myself wading in the water, dressed in red, with God's sunny face in the sky, blowing gently at first, and then with a force that parted the water so I could walk safely to the other side. Ruby told me that God made miracles happen. "Ruby," I asked, "what makes you so happy?"

"I'm talking to God, baby, just talking to God," she murmured. "Now let's get us some ice tea. I'm like to burning up." Then she whipped another shirt off the board and snapped it onto the hanger.

She unplugged the iron, wrapped the cord around the handle and from the refrigerator took the sweet tea we'd made earlier. Ruby had taught me how to open the metal ice tray with a strong jerk, removing the divider, and dropping the ice cubes one at a time into the glasses. We laughed as we sampled the slivers of ice that broke off in the tray.

"Let's make some lunch to go with our tea," she said. "Would you like to help make grilled cheese sandwiches?" Ruby never forgot what I liked.

"Yes, please," I said.

Ruby took the loaf from the breadbox and removed four slices. "Let's make three sandwiches in case a friend comes over," she said, pulling out two more slices. Ruby always planned for extra people, which my mother never did since we moved away from our relatives in St. Louis. I think she missed them; I know I did. So when Ruby made that extra sandwich, it made me believe that things could change, and that I could have friends.

She handed me the mustard jar and a knife. "Spread the mustard just so, all the way to the edges, like you always do." I felt as if I had an important job, and this made me feel smart. My brother and sister were really smart, impressing Mom with their grades, and I always felt that I needed to catch up.

I dipped my knife into the creamy mustard, plopped it onto the bread, and spread it in swirls. I took the Velveeta out of the cardboard box, opened the foil wrapping, and put the huge rectangular chunk of orange cheese onto the cutting board. Ruby let me use the cheese slicer, a silver cord with a roller and a handle.

"Not too thick now," Ruby warned as I placed the magic slicer at the top of the wedge, executed a slight flick of my wrist, and a slice of cheese fell off, the perfect match for the yellow-swathed bread on the plate. Whenever Ruby gave me a chance at something, I excelled. "What a beautiful sandwich," she would exclaim, and I would glow at her enthusiasm and her confidence in me. I wasn't sure my mother thought I could do this. But I could. I made two more sandwiches while Ruby melted the butter in a pan, and then popped in the sandwiches. She pressed them down with a spatula until they were a warm brown on the outside, with a gooey orange inside. Ruby put each sandwich on a plate and cut it in half producing two perfect triangles with cheese oozing out the sides. My mouth watered; I couldn't wait to enjoy this work of art, made even more special because it was created by my own hands.

As I was about to take a bite, the doorbell rang. I ran to answer it and found my next-door neighbor Johnny, whom I'd met the day before, when Mom and I had delivered cookies to his family.

"Can you come out and play?" he asked, looking at his feet.

I ran into the kitchen to ask Ruby, who was standing with her back to me, humming as she washed the pan and spatula. "My friend Johnny's here," I told her. "Can he stay for lunch?" I was so thrilled to think that a friend had dropped in.

"That's who the extra sandwich is for," she said, continuing her job at the sink. "It has his name on it. Go invite him in."

I ran out and took his hand. "Come on in, we're having grilled cheese sandwiches," I said, pulling him into the kitchen, smiling at Ruby, who smiled back.

Johnny froze when he saw Ruby. "I can't eat a sandwich made by a nigger," he stammered. "Mommy says they're dirty" and he ran out the door, slamming it behind him.

I didn't understand what had just happened. What was a nigger? Who was dirty? Did he mean me or Ruby? I looked at Ruby with tears in my eyes, so disappointed that my friend had left, and for reasons that made no sense to me. She put her arms around me.

"What's a nigger, Ruby?"

"It's what people call other people that are different than them" she said, her tone matter-of-fact.

"You mean because I'm a girl? He thinks I'm dirty because I'm a girl?" I couldn't believe it. It seemed so unfair.

"No, baby, it's because I'm different," she said.

"Because you're brown, is that it?" I asked, astonished.

"Yes, Precious, people are always afraid of what is different. You pay no mind. Johnny doesn't know any better. We'll eat our sandwiches and then you can go play with him. And don't you fret, because now we'll each get an extra half," she said with a wink.

"But Ruby, God is brown. I saw him up in the sky, when he parted the waters, and he looks like you." I was certain of this. I saw it in my mind and I knew it in my heart.

"God is many colors, baby, and God loves everybody the same." She handed me a plate with three crispy grilled triangles and placed an identical one in front of her. We bowed our heads as Ruby prayed: *Holy Spirit, please bless us all. Bless baby girl's family, bless Johnny's family, and bless my husband and children at home.* After a moment of silence, Ruby opened her eyes and nodded, picking up her sandwich. Together, we took our first bite. I found myself wishing I knew how to talk to God like Ruby did.

Daddy told me that night that Ruby's love of God refreshed her spirit. He said she had self-respect, and the fear and hatred of others couldn't take away her strength. Daddy said Ruby lived from a deeper truth, something eternal, and though I didn't know what eternal meant, I wanted to find out.

DO UNTO OTHERS

"Good morning, Merry Sunshine! Are you excited about our trip?" My mother leaned down and kissed my cheek. I squirmed away. Later that day, Daddy, my brother, sister and I were driving her to the station, where she would catch the train for St. Louis. She was checking into a special clinic at Barnes Hospital. Before she left, we were going to have a fried chicken dinner at the Spring Mill Inn.

I pulled the blanket over my face. I was six and I didn't want to go to Spring Mill. I didn't want to go anywhere; for fear that my mother would check into the hospital and never come home. It was 1951 and she was thirty-four.

There had been too many changes in my young life. We were now in Indiana, but that year had also found us returning to St. Louis for a second time, remaining for only three months, and then four months in Ohio, all because of Daddy's job transfer. My mother's health was now added to the upset of living in yet another new house. I often felt dizzy with fear, wondering if I would fall into a dark hole from which I might never escape.

"I'll bring back more of these special treats your aunt sent," she teased, tossing a piece of crystal mint candy into her mouth. How could she be so happy when she was facing something so scary?

When my father told me that Mom was going to a special clinic, I wondered what kind, and if this meant she was really sick. Was there something inside her that needed to be taken out?

Would there be blood? These questions seared through my brain, leaving me overwhelmed and unable to express my fears.

Looking back, I believe that Mom was lost in her own despair. She did her best to be cheerful, but she couldn't help me. I later learned that she had begun to experience the symptoms of a rare and disfiguring disease called acromegaly, characterized by the enlargement of hands and feet, as well as facial features that grow disproportionately large. As a child she had met a man whose advanced case of this disease had left him looking like a monster in her eyes. It was when she couldn't remove her wedding ring and her tongue felt too big for her mouth that she went to a doctor and was diagnosed. He referred her to the research clinic for treatment. I didn't know that the treatment was intended to stop the growth and allow her to live a normal life. Being a child, there was no way I could understand and be eased of my fear.

We wore our Sunday clothes for the drive to the train station. I was in my pressed blue dress with the starched Peter Pan collar, white socks and black patent-leather shoes. Mom sat me down in my favorite chair—a child-size wicker painted with Pennsylvania Dutch designs—and she brushed my hair. She talked about dinner while I counted the strokes, knowing she wouldn't stop until she got to one hundred. She did everything just so, and told me I was a good girl when I did, too. She liked it when I didn't spill any dirt while digging the holes in the window box for the marigolds, and when I organized the cans in the grocery cart at Kroger's market. My brother and sister were older and busy with their friends, so I was her helper.

Daddy squeezed my hand and winked as we got into the car, and I tried to keep a smile on my face. Even if my nine-year-old sister Carolyn had started an I-Spy game, or my twelve-year old brother Woody had yelled "Bryll Cream, Bryll Cream" and read those dumb posters by the side of the road, nothing could have stopped me from crying inside. As we drove, my head started to hurt and I massaged the pain. Mom gave me an aspirin, but what I really needed was to let her know that I was sad and frightened. If only she could have helped me to find the words.

I was confused about my mother's reason for leaving, but also by her behavior: she seemed glad to be leaving us. As she held the map and told Daddy where to turn, she was smiling. Did she want to get away from me? I was afraid to go to school and sometimes cried. Had I made her sick with my fear? Maybe she wanted to stay in St. Louis with her sister and never come back. My mind couldn't stop worrying.

"These are the last mints until I return," she told us, handing us the special candies her sister had sent. I felt the slick plastic wrapping covering the hard translucent ball, then I put it in my pocket, to be saved until she came home. If she came home.

The motion of the car lulled me to sleep, and I dreamed about the earth cracking open and my falling in. I woke up when we arrived at the inn.

It was noisy inside, with plates and glasses clattering. The sounds bounced around in my head, and my ears were throbbing. I ordered the children's plate and then stared at my mother. She was so beautiful, with her red lips and matching nails, her wavy brown hair and pale white skin. I wondered if this was all just a dream from which I would soon awaken.

"Please pass the butter," I said, but I must have yelled it because everybody turned to look at me. Woody and Carolyn were laughing; my parents were, too. I felt alone, as if I had no one.

"Comin' right up," my father said and we locked eyes. He grinned as he passed the butter. Those steady blue eyes made me feel safe.

After lunch, we went to see the mill, a big wood Ferris wheel with water running through it. I felt my father's arm around my shoulder.

"Penny for your thoughts," he whispered.

"Nothing," I told him. Nothing was all I felt.

When it was time to catch the train, we stood on the platform. I held my mother's hand.

"Boarding for St. Louis! Boarding for St. Louis!" shouted the platform agent.

My mother picked me up. "You be a good girl for Mommy," she said, and kissed my forehead. "I'll bring you a big bag of crystal mints."

I kissed her, trying to smile, hoping she wouldn't see my tears.

She climbed onto the train and sat at a window. She waved to us and we waved back. The train pulled away and I ran beside it, waving and shouting, "'Bye, Mommy!"

I felt myself being swept up by Daddy and saw his angry face. "What are you doing?" he demanded. "You could have been sucked under that train!" and then he hugged me so hard I almost couldn't breathe. "Don't ever scare me like that. I couldn't bear to lose you," he said. I was glad when he released his grip, and I wondered if he was afraid, too, that Mommy might not come back.

"Don't worry, Daddy," I said. "She's bringing crystal mints. She told me she would." And with a gesture that would become a lifelong habit—meeting the needs of others to distance myself from overwhelming feelings—I gave him the crystal mint, my only link to my mother's return.

MOTHER MAY I?

Rose and I were so different. Though we were both fourth graders at Tyler Elementary School in Bloomington, Indiana, I rode the bus and she lived near the school. I was chubby, with wavy blond hair, and wore dresses and saddle oxfords; she was skinny with straight black hair, and wore pants to school with penny loafers sporting dimes.

We were in the same class and both new to the school. I didn't like being new. I was shy, and was pleased when Rose introduced herself on the first day. The next week she told me that if we were going to be friends, I should come over to her house after school and play. I called my mother during lunch and she agreed to pick me up at Rose's house at four-thirty. She liked it when I made new friends. She said every family was different and it was good to be in new situations. I wasn't so sure, but I was curious. Rose seemed to want me to be her friend, and that made me feel good. I wondered what she liked about me.

When the bell rang at three-fifteen, I turned to look at Rose and saw that she was walking toward me with a smile. "Come on, let's go," she announced, strutting out of the classroom and down the hallway, pulling me along behind her. "Let's get out of here."

I had hoped to talk with Mr. Hanson about a science project I wanted to do on arrowheads, but Rose's urging told me there was no time for that. *Later* I thought, *the project can wait.*

We walked toward Rose's house and she said nothing, confidently striding ahead of me. "Isn't Mr. Hanson nice?" I offered, uncomfortable with the silence.

"Nice? How would you know? He is ugly, not handsome like his name makes out," she hissed. I felt stupid, and decided not to answer.

Rose's house was on a corner lot dotted with apple trees. At the edge of the fenced back yard was a large shed with a red door. "Is that a playhouse?" I asked as we walked down the path to her house.

"That's my step-father's workshop," she answered. I had never known anyone who had a step-father. Had her real father died? I had so many questions I wanted to ask, but instead I said, "What does he make?" I imagined beautiful wooden horses or three-story dollhouses.

"He fixes up old foreign cars. They're really expensive, so he always keeps the door locked. Come on, let's go in the house."

We were greeted at the front door by Rose's mother, a tall woman wearing tight satin capri pants, sling-back gold heels, and a black sweater. "Come on in, girls," she said. With a cigarette holder in her left hand and a glass of brown liquid in her right, she swept open the door and ushered us in. "I'll be in the kitchen, so just make yourselves at home." She had a slurry way of saying her words. Rose ignored her mother, tapping her foot as she looked out the window.

"Thank you, Mrs. Smith," I responded, as my mother had taught me.

Rose's mom laughed. "My name is Mrs. Bonart. I am not Mrs. Smith anymore, thank God."

Rose pulled me down the hallway toward her room. It was a blur of pink walls, rug and dresser. The twin beds were white, with stuffed animals surrounding the ruffled pillows. A tray with lemonade and peanut butter sandwiches rested on the bedside table.

"Help yourself," Rose chatted as she put a record on the record player. I recognized the strains of "Earth Angel." We munched and sipped as we sang along. *Earth Angel, Earth Angel, will you be mine?*

"Let's play doctor," Rose said. "I'll be the patient." She threw herself onto her bed, and unbuttoned her shirt. "Doctor, my heart is hurting, can you fix it?" she whined, tilting her head back and fluttering her eyelids. "Where is the stethoscope? You need to listen to my heart."

I looked around. I had never played this game.

"It's there on my dresser," she said, pointing.

I was surprised when she thrust her chest into the air, her tiny breasts just beginning to bloom. I got the toy stethoscope and placed it over her heart area.

"A little to the left," she purred, grabbing my hand and placing the stethoscope over her breast. She closed her eyes. "Doctor, do you think I'll be okay? Maybe I need some ointment to cure my heart. Go get some in the second drawer."

I went to her dresser, opened the second drawer and there was a bottle of Jergen's Lotion on top of her underwear. I wondered why she kept her lotion there.

"This?" I asked. My mother used Jergen's lotion for her hands and I loved the almond smell.

"Yes. Come rub it on my heart." I began to rub the Jergen's Lotion on her chest. The scent of almond was soothing and I made small circles on her chest cavity, imagining that I was healing her heart, while a funny ticklish feeling began to stir between my legs. Rose's eyes were closed and she squirmed and said, "Doctor, use your stethoscope," and I put the stethoscope on her breast like she had asked me to do before. She opened her eyes and smiled. "You're good at this."

She jumped up, buttoned her shirt and pulled me into the hallway. "Let's go play make-up in my mom's room."

I felt awkward, but followed her to the large room carpeted in white. The bed was covered by a gold bedspread and had two matching chairs and a sofa. Rose stood in a mirrored alcove with a large sit-down dressing table. On it were many bottles of perfume, and glass trays with eye shadow, pencils, powder and rouge. A hand-mirror, brush, and comb made of mother-of-pearl with silver trim were carefully placed in the center.

"Here, sit down," she said pulling out the chair. "You can use anything you want." She opened a bottle labeled *Chanel No.5* and sniffed, handing it to me. I inhaled the fragrance. "This costs one hundred dollars a bottle," she bragged.

"Wow," I said. I wondered how much my mother's *Lily of the Valley* cost. Her dressing table was tiny compared to this, and it barely fit in my parents' bedroom.

The mirror was edged with lights. I looked at myself, pretending I was a Hollywood movie star. It made me light-headed and a little dizzy; I wasn't used to being the center of attention. Rose picked up the brush and, standing behind me, ran it through my hair as she studied my face. "I'll be the mommy and you can be me," she said, and I wondered anxiously where this game would lead. I was relieved when there was a knock on the door. Her mother announced that my mother had arrived and needed to go to Kroger's before dinner. I jumped up and ran from the room.

My mother was waiting in the foyer, and I took her hand and led her out the door, calling "Bye Rose, see you tomorrow."

"Did you have a nice time?" Mom asked.

I told her it was fine, not wanting to share the details. I was aware of how comforted I was by my mother's appearance: polyester pants, a plaid shirt and tennis shoes. Her daily "mom" uniform. As we walked to the car, I felt as if I had just awakened from a bad dream. I was relieved to be out of Rose's house and back on familiar turf.

I was also comforted by the routine that I knew would follow. Mom and I would shop for dinner at Kroger's, drive home and she would prepare the food in time for my father's return from work. My brother and sister would be in their rooms doing their homework, and I would set the table. Daddy would come home at five-thirty, give Mom and me a hug, and say *How are my precious gulls* (his nickname for girls), and then pitch in to help. At six o'clock he'd put on what he called "dinner music," usually an FM classical music station, and then put the food on the plates. At the table, after saying grace, Daddy would tell us what had happened at the factory where he was the company lawyer, and talk about the union that was trying to get in, or about the workers' personal struggles, which they brought to his compassionate ear. Sometimes he and my brother would argue about politics.

Through all these evening rituals I was a quiet observer. After dinner my sister would wash the dishes, I would dry, and my brother would take out the garbage. Dad liked to rinse the pots and pans and leave them soaking in the sink to make things easier after dinner. Then we'd all go to the family room and watch the television until it was time for my bath. Bedtime was nine o'clock for me, ten for my older brother and sister. Our life seemed comfortably predictable, effortless, with few surprises.

The next day at school, Rose walked by me as if she didn't know me. When I spoke to her, she ignored me and walked over to a group of girls. She whispered something and they all looked at me, and then turned and walked away. I was crushed, but held back my tears. I had thought Rose wanted to be my friend, especially after having invited me to her house. There was a game being played but I was too naive to know the rules.

The next day, Rose was back to being friendly, and called me into the group, whispering to me about another girl, and laughing at her clothes. That became her pattern and she soon became the queen bee. I never knew whether I would be in or out of the group on any given day nor what to expect or who to trust. On the days that Rose ignored me, I arrived home from school in tears, and cried while telling my mother what had happened. Her response was always the same. "Just ignore her. And feel sorry for her that she acts that way. She is a troubled girl because her parents are divorced."

Mom didn't like it when I cried, but she would hug me and then go back to her housework. When I was hurt, I wanted her to hold me, let me cry until I stopped, and tell me everything would be fine. I wanted to be told that I would find other friends who would be loyal, and needed her to sooth my fear that there must be something wrong with me because I had trouble making friends.

It was around this time that I began staying in the classroom at recess to help Mr. Hanson. I finally understood how important it was to avoid Rose and the girls she controlled.

BLOOD SISTERS

I approached the weathered barn. I was disappointed to find it empty, with no sign of my eleven-year-old friend Emma, whom I was meeting at three o'clock. We had planned a secret ceremony.

I leaned against the sliding door and pushed its heavy weight, the familiar creaking announcing my entry. As the door opened, the dim interior came into view in frames, like negatives on a roll of film. It was the summer of 1956, and I was near Morse Pike, a country road outside the city limits of Bloomington, Indiana.

The barn was unused by its owners, the Larson family. The Larson twins, Brendan and Barton, were seventeen, like my brother, and their parents had suggested we house our new horses in the barn, since we lived only a half-mile up the road.

I entered and whistled the welcome call Daddy had taught me, a two-note repetition that sent my horse, Fleetfoot, to the edge of his stall, whinnying and hanging his head out to greet me.

I was also greeted by the tangy smell of manure, blended with the sweetness of hay, the dust it created tickling my throat. Fleet snorted, his nostrils quivering and shiny with snot, ears moving in excitement. He raised his right rear hoof, rested briefly on three legs, then lowered it, the stomp reverberating through the stall. As I stroked his snout, he threw back his head, mane flipping, then dropped it to be touched again. "Good boy," I murmured, as I scratched Fleet's chin. Yellow teeth gleamed behind black lips, as he softly nipped my hand, hoping for an apple. "Later," I told him, running my fingers through his damp and slippery mane. I cooed my affection, echoing the doves in the rafters.

"El, are you here?" I heard Emma shout. I could see her in my mind, dressed in dirty jeans from gardening, her long blonde hair in loose braids. She always seemed comfortable with herself, not shy like me.

"I'm here with Fleet," I called back. "Come on over."

My thoughts turned to the first time I met Emma.

When I was ten, Daddy and I were out horseback riding and stopped to introduce ourselves to a woman and girl who were weeding the garden at their new house, up the hill from the barn. The girl's name was Emma. Her mom told us that when she saw the horses, she'd thought we were rednecks from the Ku Klux Klan. Daddy frowned and said, "Let's hope we never see those evil murderers in these parts." A lawyer, he was passionate about right and wrong, but unlike Emma's parents, his politics were conservative. My brother once said the Klan wouldn't come near our liberal university town, even though their headquarters were in South Bend, two hours north of Bloomington. I didn't know who the Klan had killed or why they were on the loose, but I thought maybe they had escaped from jail in South Bend.

Emma had stood back from the horses. She seemed frightened, but carried on a conversation with my dad, asking questions. I found it odd that she could be afraid of horses but comfortable talking with my dad, at the same time playing with her cat, who had jumped onto her shoulder, hissing and clawing. That cat scared me. I figured fear came out when a person saw something they weren't used to.

"I've got the grapevines," Emma called to me, referring to our plan to smoke them ceremonially as part of the secret ritual she had planned. She smiled, walked past me, and began climbing the ladder to the hayloft. "Bren and Bart were pruning their parents' grapevines last week and they gave me two branches. I cut the vines into six inch sticks, left them in the sun, and now they're dry as a bone." We had agreed that if the boys were old enough to smoke cigarettes, we were old enough to create our own version.

A lot of things had led up to this day. Bren and Bart lived across the field, south of the barn, in a nineteenth century white clapboard house that had served as a way station for the Underground Railroad. Emma had explained that there wasn't really a train under the ground, but a safe house for slaves escaping from owners who bought and sold slaves like cattle, whipping them to exhaustion in the cotton fields. I'd never heard that kind of talk in my home.

The twins loved history and seemed proud of their old farmhouse. Their father, like Emma's, was a professor at Indiana University. The first time I saw the house, I noticed descending stone steps at the back, overhung by a thick lilac bush and leading to a basement door. I wondered if this was where the slaves had entered to sleep during the day, so they could continue their travels at night.

In Girl Scouts, Emma and I sang "Follow The Drinkin' Gourd" and learned about how Harriet Tubman, a runaway slave herself, had led groups north in secrecy, guided by the North Star in the Big Dipper. Emma said that Harriet carried a gun she never used. It was a reminder to any fugitive who became too frightened to keep running that slavery was death, and freedom the only life worth living.

I thought Harriet was as brave as any man. I imagined her with beams of starlight surrounding her as she traveled through Indiana, risking her life for the freedom of others. Emma and I decided to form a club and call ourselves The Freedom Sisters in honor of Harriet. Our theme song was "Follow the Drinkin' Gourd." We had regular meetings where we talked about our dream of being courageous and helping others to be free.

My history book mentioned Harriet Tubman, but I don't remember any discussion of the Ku Klux Klan. Once, when I was walking home from the barn, I came upon Bren reading in the field of Queen Ann's Lace behind his house. He showed me a picture of Klansmen on their horses, carrying torches, and wearing white robes, pointed hats and ghost-like face coverings with circular eye-holes. He said the Klan hanged black men from trees and burned down their houses. It was then that I realized the Klan lived among us.

As I listened to Bren, an image appeared in my mind of the only black person I had ever known. It was Ruby, our beloved housekeeper when I was six and living in Ohio. She had a grown son, Charles, and I wondered if Charles had been one of the Klan's victims.

I couldn't get Ruby's face out of my mind. I imagined her lying at the base of a tree, sobbing, her house behind her in smoldering ashes, the feet of her son dangling above her.

I felt shattered by this image, and began to wonder how it must feel to live in constant fear. I wished I could ask a friend, but there were no black children at my school. I began to grasp that freedom from slavery did not mean that black people were free. I felt sick at my stomach, the helpless nausea of a young girl on whom the awareness of racial hatred was dawning. It was as if I had one piece to a terrifying puzzle and no way to make sense of the scramble of shapes that lay before me. Since no one at home was talking about the Klan's awful deeds, I didn't ask. When I told Emma what I felt, she suggested that we perform a secret ritual at our upcoming meeting of the Freedom Sisters, and I agreed, even though I didn't know what to expect.

I was about to find out what Emma had in mind. I followed her with anticipation to the empty hayloft and sat cross-legged on the floor. She sat across from me and placed a tin box between us, opened the lid and went through the contents for me to see. She said nothing, but I knew she would explain soon enough. There was a book of matches, a safety pin, six grapevine sticks, two cotton balls, a pencil and a piece of paper, all of which she put back in the box.

"Here's the plan," Emma began. "First we become blood sisters. As the Freedom Sisters, our motto is *Crush the Ku Klux Klan*. This is our secret and not even the twins can know about it."

This was not the first time we discussed what our motto would be. The Klan were monsters who needed to be disempowered in our young minds, especially if we were to sustain the hope of helping others. We wanted to be brave and strong and fight heroic battles, even though our mothers didn't have the same dreams for us.

My mother's life revolved around our family and our home, and though I was expected to be like her, I wasn't. For one thing, I wanted to change the world beyond my family. I imagined riding Fleet all the way to the Pacific Ocean without fear of being stopped. I wanted to find a way for everyone to be free and unafraid. Crushing the Ku Klux Klan seemed like a place to start, even if only in my fantasies. At eleven I believed that anything was possible.

I nodded, closing my eyes to show my solemnity.

"At the end," she continued, "we smoke the grapevines to celebrate our bond. So let's get started." She opened the safety pin, lit a match, and placed it at the end of the pin. "That's to sterilize it," she said, as she blew out the match and touched it to her tongue. "Do you want me to go first?"

"Yes," I whispered in the hush of hayloft, thrilled by the importance of what we were about to do.

She opened her left hand, and with her thumb, pushed the flesh of her middle finger to the tip, then pricked it with the safety pin. Blood spotted her finger.

"Your turn," she said, and I followed her lead, drawing blood as quickly as she had done. She took my hand and pressed our fingers together. "Now the Freedom Sisters are blood sisters." We nodded in agreement. She pulled the paper out of the box and pushed her finger against it, making a mark in blood. I did the same.

"Blood sisters for life," she wrote, and we signed our names and the date: June 15, 1956. As we pressed the cotton against our fingers, I felt relieved, sensing that our ritual had power, though not knowing how or why.

"Now for the grapevines," Emma announced. She took one of the sticks, struck a match, and held it under the tip of the twig until it was a glowing ember. "Be careful with the ash," she warned, "and keep it over the tin box." I again repeated her actions, confident that she knew what she was doing. We brought the other end of the grapevines to our lips and sucked. Looking at each other, we collapsed into giggles. The grapevines went out almost immediately, which we hardly noticed.

As our laughter dissipated and we sat in silence, I began to wonder about how people became evil. I remembered Ruby telling me that hatred came from fear. I thought about how Emma was afraid of horses and I was afraid of cats, mostly because we had never been around them. I didn't know any black people besides Ruby, but I had no reason to hate them. Why were the Klan so afraid of dark skin? How could they believe they had the right to kill someone? Did they think they were better than other people? These questions stayed with me.

I heard Fleet whinny.

"Someone's coming," I said. I stood up, preparing to leave. We tossed everything into the tin box and climbed down the ladder, Emma clutching the box under her shirt. As we slipped out the door, I thought about the freedom I felt when I rode through the fields on Fleet, imagining that we were part of a wild herd. I pictured us stampeding the Klan, crushing them until they were dust, and freeing their horses for a better life.

Though Emma and I eventually moved apart, the image of the tin box, holding the document of our intention, was carried in my heart as I grew up. It was my reminder that I was on the side of justice and change.

When I look at the stars, I imagine Harriet Tubman riding her wild steed through the sparkling night sky, resting for a moment in the vessel of the big dipper, then charging forward again, ivory pistol at her side, reminding me not to stray from the path of freedom or retreat when fear overwhelms me. I can almost hear her singing:

Follow the drinkin' gourd, we gonna
Follow the drinkin'gourd,
Keep on traveling' that muddy road to freedom
Follow the drinkin' gourd.

EXPOSURE

It was the Fall of 1958. Emma and I were walking on the Indiana University campus, two thirteen-year-olds, feeling the thrill of independence. Emma was wearing blue jeans and a loose blue Indiana University t-shirt; I was in matching green pedal-pushers and polo shirt. Her father was an English professor and we were walking to his office for lunch. We planned to go to the fifth floor Physiology Department after lunch to see if we could peek at the cadavers stored there by the medical students.

"Dad's taking us to lunch at the student union at noon," said Emma. "We're a little early, so we still have time to explore."

The campus had wooded trails and creeks, its maple, beech and oak trees creating a serene environment, one where our parents believed we were safe. We knew the campus by heart; we had been exploring it for years.

"Let's go by the Art Building and play in the Venus fountain," I suggested. It was Indian summer, meaning we could wade in the shallow water and pick up coins that had accumulated in the clamshell from which the goddess emerged.

As we wove our way from the trail to the sidewalk that ran alongside a campus roadway, we walked and skipped and giggled our delight. A loud knock distracted us. I looked up to a second floor window and saw a man standing there. He was staring at us. His pants were unzipped and his huge penis swung from side to side as he beckoned to us.

"What is that man doing," I asked Emma.

"He's just one of those guys who plays with himself all the time," Emma said, as she casually flipped her hand in the air. She knew things I didn't. She had once told me about the Kinsey Reports, studies done at Indiana University years earlier. They suggested that "normal" sex was a myth. Emma didn't give details and I didn't want to know. Later, my brother said that he heard how professors' kids got an eyeful when they snuck around at their parents' parties, even though Emma denied that she had done anything other than play Scrabble at these dinners.

"But he's smiling that creepy smile and motioning for us to come," I whispered. My heart was racing, yet I couldn't take my eyes off this frightening man, fearful he would suddenly appear besides us and snatch me away.

"He's harmless, El. Stop worrying." Emma was convincing, but I still felt sick to my stomach. I had never seen a fully exposed penis; my father and brother sometimes walked around the house in their boxer shorts, never naked. Did they ever pull it out for others to see? I cringed at the thought of my dad or brother scaring me in this way.

"I think he might be dangerous," I said. "Don't you think we should tell someone?"

"Of course not. He's just a lonely guy having a little fun."

I heard the knock again and, despite trying not to look, I couldn't help myself. This time he was holding money, beckoning for us to take it. I stood motionless and stared, while Emma ran ahead yelling "Race you to the fountain!"

I heard a chirping sound and saw a robin returning to the nest with a worm for her babies crying out in hunger. I felt stuck, as if my feet were in dried cement. A breeze cooled my face as I tried to focus on the activity in the branches of the giant maple. I knew that my fears were real and I felt sad that Emma didn't understand. I also felt ashamed that I had seen something that was supposed to be private.

I looked at the window and the man was gone. My feet began to move before I was aware that I was running to catch up with Emma. I glanced back to be sure he wasn't chasing me, intent on either giving me the money or hurting me. It reminded me of the time my father explained to my older sister that girls who wore short skirts or low-necked blouses gave a bad impression. I didn't know what "a bad impression" was, but I did know that I didn't want to be bad.

By the time I reached the fountain, the pounding of my shoes on the pavement and the effort to run away had made me feel better. Emma and I continued on as if nothing had happened. After lunch, I told her I didn't want to see the cadavers after all. I had seen enough nudity for one day and didn't need to be frightened yet again.

That night, as I undressed for my bath, I caught a glimpse of myself in the mirror. My chest was so flat I didn't even need a training bra, so how could I have looked like a woman to that man? I couldn't imagine that I did, and yet why would the man show me his private parts and smile at me? I decided to tell my mother about what had happened.

When she came in to say goodnight, I began to cry. She hugged me and kissed my forehead as she always did, and asked me what was wrong.

"Emma and I saw a man in a window today, and I was scared," I said.

"What scared you?"

"He had his pants unzipped and he was moving his penis around." We had been taught to use anatomical terms instead of silly names.

"Where was this?" she asked, concern in her voice.

I told her about the student union, and how he crooked his finger at me like he wanted me to come inside. "Emma ran away," I added, "and I couldn't move. Then he waved money at me. I was so afraid. When I looked up again, he wasn't there." By this time I was sobbing. My mother continued to hold me, soothing me until I settled down. I wanted to tell her about how frightened and ashamed I was, but I couldn't find the words. A familiar longing to be heard, to be understood, rose up within me, but I was consumed by a silence I couldn't broach.

"He was a sick man," my mother explained. "And what he did was wrong. I am sorry he frightened you. Now go on to sleep and forget all about it." Forgetting was her way, something she had learned to help her cope. And I had learned that it was my job to help her.

I rolled over and closed my eyes, as if I were asleep. I finally dozed off, but I carried that terrifying image of the man in the window for many years, as I carried the pain of being unable to connect with my mother whenever I was afraid.

GOT YOUR BACK

In the ninth grade, everything changed. It was 1959, I was starting high school, and I fell in love with Ricky Nelson. He became a star the first time he sang on *Ozzie and Harriet*. I played his single "Poor Little Fool" on my RCA 45 record player, swaying with the music and imagining his eyes looking into mine. He sang to me about his sadness at being jilted, which filled me with empathy and excitement. I nearly fainted from the connection to his voice.

My friends who bad-mouthed President Ike and capitalism—sounding very much like their professor parents—and talked about where they wanted to go to college, didn't understand my infatuation with the teenage heartthrob, and insisted that it was stupid. I no longer fit in with them, so I made new friends with the girls who were boy-crazy like me. My best friend, Marla, had just moved to my neighborhood and we were invited to slumber parties held by the popular girls with big houses. These gatherings focused on Ricky Nelson records. We screamed and swooned as we danced and shouted out our fantasies about being Ricky's girl.

Marla and I got right into it, but we were careful to keep our distance from the mean girls in the group, the ones who gossiped and bullied for status. These were the same girls who dominated the hallways at school. So we stuck together, deciding each night what to wear to school the next day and giving each other advice on hair and make-up. When two boys on the basketball team invited us to double date to the movies, we accepted. They had seen us in the school canteen where they fed nickels to the jukebox during lunch. When Marla heard The Everly Brothers singing "Bye-Bye Love," she pulled me onto the dance floor and we jitterbugged. That's when they invited us out. My date, Hoot, was tall and lanky with black hair and eyes, and olive skin. When he played basketball he was smooth on the court, but usually ignored the girls who tried to talk to him after the games.

In the theater, Hoot put his arm around me. As we were walking, he kissed me quickly on the cheek. I felt myself blush, but he kept walking as if nothing had happened.

The four of us went to his parents' house and I felt that familiar Ricky Nelson swoony feeling when Hoot took my hand and pulled me down next to him on the sofa. He didn't have much to say, so we listened to Johnny Mathis records and he kissed me on the mouth. Playing Spin the Bottle was my only kissing experience and this didn't feel like that. With this kiss, my face tingled and my heartbeat quickened. He didn't stop after one kiss. He pulled my face toward his and pushed his tongue into my mouth. I could hardly breathe and wondered if this was what the popular girls called *making out*. I tried to wiggle away, but his grip was strong and he ignored me. When he reached inside my blouse and grabbed my breast, I yanked my head back, and said, "Stop."

"Come on, you know you like this," he whispered in my ear.

A rush of anger blazed across my face. "No, I don't," I said and stood up.

Marla and Jimmy were at the other end of the couch and they were kissing. She looked up, and I mouthed *bathroom*. She scooted off the sofa and we walked down the hall, closing the door behind us. I told her what had happened. We agreed it was time to call my father and get a ride home.

We called from the kitchen and returned to the boys who were watching television. I told Hoot we had to go home, but he ignored us. Jimmy walked us to the porch and waited silently. As the car pulled up to the curb, he looked down and mumbled, "I'm sorry." Then he accompanied us to the car, opened the door, and said, "Hi, Mr. Woods."

I didn't mention to Daddy what had happened, but I'm certain he would have been furious at Hoot and probably would have sat him down for a talk about being a teenage boy and respecting teenage girls.

On Monday, I trudged up three flights of stairs with my fellow freshmen. Hoot and his buddies were congregated near the radiator, checking out the girls. I quickly scanned the line-up: Hoot on the left, sitting on the radiator and leaning his elbows on the windowsill, stretching his legs in front of him. Jimmy stood beside him, head down, hands in his pockets. My friend Joe John and his teammate Tommy completed the line up, talking and laughing, and both looking cool in their football jackets.

Hoot glared at me as I turned toward my homeroom. I acted as if I didn't see him, feeling confident in my mint-green dyed-to-match pleated skirt and angora sweater. My hair was freshly washed and in a ponytail, my lipstick and mascara just so. With saddle shoes and white socks, the outfit was complete.

"Bitch," he hissed, and my face flushed. I sped up, hoping my tears wouldn't cause my mascara to run. I heard footsteps behind me and I nearly froze when I felt an arm around my shoulder.

"It's me, Ellen," said Joe John. "Are you okay?"

My shoulders shook as I silently cried. Joe John led me into an empty room, and with his hands on my shoulders, looked at me with concern in his eyes.

"I know why he said that," I said. "He hates me because I said no to him."

"Well, that's his problem," Joe John replied. "What he said was wrong. No girl should be talked to like that."

I felt relief and gratitude that Joe John was on my side. "What if people heard what he said?"

"He's a bully, but don't worry. I'll make sure he leaves you alone." Joe John was the captain of the basketball team, a position coveted by Hoot, and I wondered what he was going to do.

When I looked up at him, he smiled and said, "You sure do look pretty. You brighten up my day."

I managed to return the smile and rub tears off my face. "Thank you," I murmured, too shy to know what else to say.

The hallway was crowded and noisy with students slamming their lockers and shouting lunch plans to each other as they scurried into their classrooms.

"Will you have lunch with me?" Joe John asked. "We can take our lunchboxes out to the football field and sit in the bleachers." When I told him I'd like that, he added "I'll meet you outside Chemistry class."

I wondered how he knew that I had Chemistry before lunch.

Joe John and I had been friends since Junior High. In the eighth grade we were in the same homeroom and sometimes did our homework together. He helped me with math and I helped him with his English papers. His father had died of a heart attack that year and he told me how hard it was for his mother, who continued to work full time. He worried about her, and got a weekend job to help support the family. Sometimes his tears broke through when he talked about it, but he tried to put his emotions into sports. Joe John played football, basketball and baseball, and he excelled at all of them.

Joe John was waiting outside the door as he had promised. He took my books and we walked toward my locker. "I looked at the class lists early this morning," he said. "That's how I knew you were in Chemistry."

"You really are watching out for me, aren't you?" I told him, feeling surprisingly flirtatious with this boy who'd I'd always thought of like a brother.

He handed me my books, which I shoved in the locker, and then I pulled out my lunchbox. "With guys like Hoot around, you bet I am," he said. "I told him that if he ever said anything like what he said this morning, he'd have to answer to me. I think he heard me."

His reminder of the incident made me clench up. I felt his hand against my back, and I almost relaxed. We walked silently to the football field and sat in the bleachers eating our sandwiches and milk. He told me about the upcoming football game and we chatted about the players.

As we closed our lunchboxes and prepared to go back to class, Hoot appeared before us. He stood there, staring at us with such intensity that Joe John put his arm around me.

"You have something to say, Hoot?" he asked calmly. "Go ahead and say it."

Hoot sniffed and tossed his head back, then mumbled, "I'm sorry."

"Who are you talking to? We can't hear you," Joe John urged.

"I'm talking to Ellen and I said I'm sorry. It won't happen again."

I sat there staring at Joe John as Hoot walked away. "Did you make him do that?" I asked. I couldn't believe anybody could get through to Hoot.

"For you I'd do anything," he grinned. "C'mon, let's not be late to class." He took my hand and we walked.

It wasn't long after that when Joe John told me he'd been in love with me since the eighth grade. We went steady throughout high school and he even talked about marriage. As time went on, I knew that our goals were different: I wanted a career and he wanted a wife. At graduation, we parted ways, but I have never forgotten the boy who had my back and my heart in high school.

COURTLY LOVE

I walked out on sorority life six months after joining. I was angry that they refused to accept Jewish girls, and they wouldn't even discuss taking a top student because she wore green cat-eye glasses with rhinestones. The last thing I wanted was to live with my parents, so I began working as a waitress; it was the only way I could afford an apartment. I found a basement apartment—actually, two beds in a cubicle, with a tiny kitchen and living area—and rented it with Verbena, another English major. She was a senior who had long flowing hair, wore gauzy tunics and sandals, and was writing her thesis on Courtly Love, which she explained was the Medieval view of love where a woman was idealized and served as inspiration for a man's creativity. I was intrigued.

I was focused on my Art minor, and spent my free time taking photographs for an introductory photography course. I liked to capture the theme of abandonment in various forms: human faces, empty structures, and overgrown landscapes. My teacher said the images were sentimental, that I needed to find more original expressions. He was an overweight bald man in his late forties and was known to photograph his female students in the nude, explaining that such vulnerability inspired their work. Although he never proposed this to me, I began to photograph myself in the nude, using a self-timer on a tripod. I hiked alone to an isolated forest I knew from my childhood, an area with rocky creeks surrounded by sycamores, and beds of thick ferns and fallen trees overrun with wildflowers. After capturing myself on film, head turned away from the lens, I liked to rest on a boulder and read Walt Whitman's *Song of Myself*, which I always carried. I was enlivened by these solitary forays into the forest and proud of my final presentation of photographs. The instructor shared my enthusiasm: I received an A+.

Stark, who was a lanky blonde and a fellow student, introduced himself on the last day of class. He asked if he could give me a ride on his bicycle to the Student Union, where he'd seen me studying. I was surprised that he knew who I was, and a little embarrassed that I hadn't noticed him. But I was curious, so I accepted his offer. I sat on the cross bar and he maneuvered the sidewalk, while telling me that, in addition to taking photographs, he wrote poetry. I learned that he lived on the town square and that his room was above the music store, where he strung guitars in exchange for rent and access to the pot of soup regularly simmering on the hot plate in the back of the store. He said he got free day-old bread at the bakery, and he sometimes lifted a bottle of wine from the liquor store. His bike, which he called Steiglitz, had been spray painted green immediately after he stole it from a fraternity house. I had grown up in a law-abiding conservative family; I found his lifestyle strangely appealing.

Stark began to join me when I studied on campus. He would sit beside me, rubbing my neck and back and sometimes unzipping the back of my dress to "get more traction skin to skin." He said my hair was like silk and my face radiated with ethereal grace. He read his poetry to me and called me his muse. When we parted he usually pecked at my lips several times, one hand behind my head and the other running through my hair. "Beautiful," he'd say. He never called me by name.

I felt self-conscious with Stark, and not connected. It was as if we were actors playing our parts. When he told me he wanted to make love to me I began to wonder if that was what was missing. I told him I'd never had intercourse, and he replied "Beautiful, I'll be your first." I had been taught to save myself for marriage. I was changing in so many ways, but I figured *why not*, which was fine with him. It seemed so simple.

Stark planned our tryst. He scheduled it for a Monday at two in the afternoon, while it was still light. "I want to see you," he said.

He led me up to his room, a space framed like an attic, without walls. It was bathed in bronze light streaming in through a solitary skylight. Hanging from the ceiling were Indian bedspreads, which he pushed aside so I could enter a space big enough for a double mattress covered with a white sheet. He lit a candle and silently began to undress me. I stood there awkwardly, as if I was somewhere else and watching the scene unfold. He unhooked my bra and it dropped to the floor. He gazed at my breasts and murmured, "Beautiful." He pulled down my panties and asked me to lie on the bed, while he prepared the birth control, something I hadn't even considered. It was a green spermicidal gel that he squeezed into a six-inch tube and then asked me to spread my legs so he could inject it. "So we'll be safe," he said. I felt like I was at the doctor's office being treated for a disease, wondering if this was the way it was usually done. But, as with the doctor, I asked no questions, made no comments, but observed quietly, leaving the process of thinking about this until later.

I knew about sex from the passionate make-out sessions I had engaged in regularly with my high school boyfriend, who was my first love. He had taught me about my body and his in a way that was both romantic and exciting, and left me feeling valued.

As we made love, Stark was like a stranger going through a ritual that didn't include me. He lay on top of me and moved his hips around until he got hard.

"I'm going in now," he said, like a reporter about to enter an extreme weather zone. I imagined his penis entering a dark cave filled with green spermicide, looking for a place to explore. "How does it feel? Are you okay?" he said in a throaty voice. "Does it hurt?"

It did hurt a bit, but I decided to act as if it didn't. "No, I'm fine," I said, hoping it would be over soon. Where were the surges of energy and longing I had felt with my high school boyfriend?

As he thrust his hips, he gave details of his journey into my cave. "Oh, it's so warm in here," he crooned. "Nice. Very nice." His normally receding jaw jutted forward and his eyes were briefly closed. After a moment, he checked in again. "Are you okay?"

I told him I was, which was his signal to begin thrusting and huffing and diving into me, pinning my hands down with his, until he heaved one last grunt, then pulled himself out. "Yes. Beautiful," he announced. "That was beautiful." I had no idea what he was talking about. How could minor pain, a smothering sensation from his weight atop me, and a greasy goo in my crotch be beautiful?

"You're awfully quiet," he said. "Was I too rough?"

"No, I'm fine," I assured him.

He patted my butt, rolled over, and began snoring softly.

Thrilled to be free, I got up, put on my clothes, and ran down the stairs. I walked as fast as I could to my apartment, imagining what Verbena would say when I told her the details. Love didn't seem to be a part of what I'd just been through, but maybe Stark was inspired by it. Maybe this was courtly love.

If so, it left a lot to be desired. I began considering a move to California.

GATEWAY

The morning air was filled with suspended droplets as the fog rolled in from the ocean. I stepped out of my apartment door and onto the marble landing, and checked the reflection of my hair in the brass nameplate boasting "Falmouth Arms." Only my big brother would think to rename it "Disarming Foulmouth," in honor of the Free Speech movement that had erupted at UC Berkeley across the bay.

It was the summer of 1967 and I had arrived in San Francisco from Indiana three weeks earlier, age twenty-two and thrilled to begin a new life. This was my first official date with Gerry. We had spent two weekends together in the company of our brothers, neighbors who had introduced us, but this was our first time alone. Gerry had warned me, "It will be an out-of-body experience, and that's all I'm going to tell you."

The motorcycle pulled up. Gerry was wearing a gleaming black helmet that covered his curly Semitic-brown hair. He smoothly backed into the curb, lifted the bike up on the kickstand, and swung his leg over to dismount. He was my height, five-five, and I felt drawn to his stocky body and his sure hands. He bounded up the stairs with the greeting, "Are you ready for this?" He knew I had never been on a motorcycle.

"Ready and waiting." I smiled as he took my elbow and walked me down the steps, our gaits synchronizing instantly. I've often thought that was the moment I fell in love. There was something about being with him that was natural, familiar, and easy.

"Let me help you." He pushed my long hair behind my ears, pulled a second helmet off the handlebars, and placed it on my head, snapping the strap under my chin.

I felt strangely dizzy, but I liked it, and climbed onto the seat behind him.

"Just put your arms around my waist and hold on tight," he told me. "I promise to drive safely."

As we sped along, I found myself shouting a silly riddle I'd heard in Indiana. "How can you recognize a happy motorcyclist?"

"By the bugs in his teeth," he laughed, not missing a beat.

Riding through San Francisco, I quickly lost track of where we were. My experience was centered on the man whose back was pressed against me. I felt the bulk of his body as I held on, inhaling the tang of leather, and the Ivory Soap smell of his neck. I watched the rainbow of Victorian houses whiz by, the landscape changing as we passed through different neighborhoods.

"This is Chinatown. Can you smell the food?" His voice was deep enough to be distinguished from the din around us.

"Hot and Sour Soup," I said, nearly shouting. It was my favorite.

"That would make a good lunch, my favorite."

Bingo.

We drove on until we came to a massive flame-colored structure gracefully looming in front of us.

"Isn't this amazing?" he asked, the Golden Gate Bridge now in full view. The wind had picked up and the salty ocean smell was unmistakable.

I stretched my neck to speak into his ear. "Yes!" I felt his cheek lift in a smile.

We drove past the few solitary runners, windbreakers puffed with air as the men and women paced themselves, arms bent, fists closed. Did they even notice the ocean and the glowing towers? Contentment washed over me, my face warmed by the sun resting midway to noon in the clear sky. "I see what you mean by an out-of-body experience." I leaned back to take in the vastness of the sky merging with the boundless ocean.

Gerry pulled into the lookout stop at the north end of the bridge and we walked closer to the water. "It affects me the same way every time," he said. "I know everything will be okay when I'm breathing ocean air. That's why I wanted to come here with you."

I felt suddenly shy, unable to speak.

"How are you feeling?" he continued. "Have you returned to your body?" His face was flushed as his eyes explored mine.

"I don't remember ever feeling this good. Is that in body or out of body?" I ventured.

"It's just the beauty of it all; it opens us up to something larger than ourselves." The wind surged around us. "I like you." His brown eyes were steady.

I couldn't look away. "I like you, too." Hadn't I known this man forever? Our connection was undeniable.

He took my hand and we walked back to the motorcycle. On our way, I supposed, to the next adventure. And there would be many.

Eight months later, Gerry was dead and I was flattened, as if I, too, had died. The grief was so shattering that I was incapable of feeling it. I had no idea how I would fill the hole in my life, not knowing how immense that hole would be or how his death would determine the course my life would take.

BLACK POWER

After Gerry's suicide, I couldn't imagine how I would complete my final semester. It rained almost every day for a month and I walked the gloomy streets around UC Berkeley, soothed only by the occasional burst of purple-flowered shrubbery against white stucco. The contrast created a mirage of joy, a momentary lightness of spirit.

Tears and rain washed over me. I imagined Gerry miraculously returning, and I was unable to allow myself to feel the despair that hovered inside. Instead, my feelings arrived in flashes. I had lost a profound connection to someone I loved, and lost a connection to myself as well. Emotionally paralyzed, I struggled to complete my classes.

I finally pulled myself together and delivered my senior thesis on "Song of Myself: The Photograph as Poem." This was a collection of the woodland self-portraits I had taken the year before, and they were interspersed with quotes from Walt Whitman. I received a grade of C, which allowed me to graduate that Spring semester.

Following graduation, I entered a kind of dissociated state. I felt shut down, and spent my time drinking espresso and writing in my journal about my plans for the future. I was unable to submerge myself in the grief that threatened to overwhelm me. Working as a waitress at night, I became a daytime fixture at a café across from Boalt Hall, the university's law school, which was a short walk to International House, a building of student apartments where Gerry had lived and died. The caffeine was like an elixir to my grief, elevating my mood and reinforcing my denial. Soon, I felt surprisingly grounded and able to engage with the world.

Within a month, I was courted, swept away and then proposed to by Martin, a law student. He was unlike any man I'd ever known. His interest in law felt familiar, since my father and brother were both lawyers. But Martin was prep school and Harvard educated, and he possessed an unusual mix of pretense and humility that I found attractive. He loved classical music, which drove him to break out occasionally into conducting gestures, especially when he heard or even thought about a moving piece of music. He recognized and brought out my adventurous spirit, and he admired my love of simplicity and Nature. Martin told me that he had fallen hopelessly in love with me when we first met, and all he wanted was to make me happy.

Martin introduced me to his family on May Day, at a gathering at his sister's home in the wealthy coastal town of Carmel. She grilled me on my interests and plans, and alluded to the fact that I didn't possess the Ivy League or trust-fund credentials that qualified me for the family name. Martin told me to ignore her, explaining that she was a busybody and over protective. But in the end, he was unable to stand up to his wealthy parents from the elite enclave of Atherton, who'd been charming but cold during our visit.

His father was a vice president at Chevron, and invited us to visit him at his company's penthouse office in the San Francisco financial district. After we arrived, I was left in the waiting room while he conferred with his son about his inheritance and the kind of woman he needed to marry. He provided Martin with a round-trip ticket to Munich for the summer, which he reluctantly accepted. Though Martin begged me to wait for his return, I did not, deeply disappointed by his inability to stand up to his father and choose me over his family's money.

I increased my hours at my waitress job. I also took a second job substituting as a teacher's aide at the burgeoning Head Start Early Childhood Education program in West Oakland, a black ghetto a few miles from my student apartment. The program's site was a portable classroom on a concrete slab, with an aging jungle gym, slide and swings competing for space in a play area enclosed by a chain link fence; the only color came from dying vines. The children were delivered daily by family members and were provided a breakfast of milk and soda crackers, eked out of the teachers' personal budgets. My co-worker, Alicia, had a son who was paralyzed after being hit by a stray bullet in a police shootout in her neighborhood, just blocks from the school. When she told me about the children who had lost parents from police violence, I felt angry and powerless.

My eyes were beginning to open and my hopes of finding a way to introduce preschoolers to poetry were subsumed by my growing awareness of the poverty and violence in the community. Martin Luther King's recent murder and the reality of the lives of these children were shocking revelations. Perhaps non-violence was not the only way to right these wrongs.

A familiar longing for change arose in me. I had often felt an affinity with people who had been mistreated. Memories of being an outsider in my family, in school, and in relationships developed into a pressure to act. I wanted to be more than a witness to the effects of violence. I was alone, and I longed to be a part of a community of people who were changing history.

The Black Panthers Party for Self-Defense, organized by Huey Newton and Bobby Seale, was a visible presence. It was the summer of 1968 and the group formed at Merritt College, an Oakland community college adjacent to my Berkeley neighborhood. They advocated for change through their Ten-Point Program, demanding, among other things, freedom and self-determination, full employment and housing, truthful education about black history, and an end to police brutality. As I rode the bus to work, I saw members on the street corners in front of the college, selling the Black Panther Party newspaper. The men were dressed in black, leather jackets and berets almost shimmering with intensity as calls for "Power to the People" thundered through the crowds that formed around them.

I bought their paper. The next day, I went to a large gathering at UC Berkeley, joining young people of all races. We listened to Huey Newton and Bobby Seale speak about freedom and justice; I raised my fist and shouted the chants, feeling an urgency to be a part of the movement. The energy made me feel alive, committed and hopeful. Huey and Bobby addressed the growing crowds with passion about racism and the need for self-defense. I had read about the Panther's dedication to protecting their people *by any means necessary*, and I began to understand and embrace their messages. It was a solitary time in my life, and I rarely talked to anyone about these thoughts.

One July day in 1968, I saw a group of around thirty Black Panthers standing in military formation in front of Merritt College, rifles across their chests. They were holding a banner emblazoned with "Free Huey. Rally Tomorrow." I didn't know what had happened, but I was in awe of their strength and their loyalty to their people. That day, a stranger on the bus told me that the Panthers monitored policemen. They also monitored arrests in their communities, and worked to bail people out and get them legal representation.

All of this information exposed a nerve in me. I remembered witnessing racial hatred as a child, and as a pre-teen seeing pictures of the Ku Klux Klan in my home state of Indiana, where they maintained their headquarters. I had heard of their horrifying acts of violence for years, and now a deep rage about inequality began to stir in me. I learned more about the abuses of civil rights still rampant in the lives of black people in Oakland. Through Gerry's death and my disappointment in Martin, I had lost sight of the atrocities in the local community.

There were times when I thought how my ignorance made me complicit. Hearing Huey Newton and Bobby Seale speak so eloquently brought my life back into focus. Equality and justice became driving forces in my emerging identity.

News reports announced that Huey Newton had been indicted by a grand jury for the murder of a police officer. I attended the rally that prepared participants to carry "Free Huey" signs and march to the Alameda County Courthouse where the trial would be held. We arrived at the appointed time, held our signs high, thrust our clenched fists skyward as we stood across from the courthouse, a limestone edifice occupying a full city block. Standing above us, Bobby Seale and other Panther leaders maintained order.

When I heard that attendance at the trial was open to the public, I joined other supporters. We pushed into the courtroom with determination, a ritual that would be repeated daily. Sitting shoulder to shoulder with white radicals and black activists, I felt engaged and focused in a way I had never been in college. Not only was I learning about the sinister ways that racism limited the freedom of blacks, I also learned how jury selection was often a sham, and that "a jury of one's peers" was an impossibility for black people.

Huey Newton was represented by Charles Garry, a well-known civil rights attorney and Armenian immigrant who skillfully used witnesses, drawings and enactments to show Huey's innocence, while reinforcing how unlikely it was for him to get a fair trial. Garry was so unrelenting in his cross-examination that one police officer jumped out of the witness box and threatened to pull his gun on Garry, who stepped aside, raising his palms to indicate that his point about police brutality had indeed been made. I was riveted. Charles Garry's brilliant voice for the oppressed spoke directly to my heart. Though Huey was convicted of a lesser charge in that trial, and would spend two years in jail, the appeal resulted in a hung jury, and Huey would eventually be freed.

After the first trial was over, I was so enamored with the law that I briefly considered law school, but instead chose a job as a legal secretary in a collective of radical white lawyers. I did legal work for many years as well as community organizing to support the election of black leaders to political office.

THE POWER OF SISTERHOOD

"Jenny told me you're gay," I blurted. "I've never met a lesbian before! So if I seem nervous, just know it's not you, it's me."

It was 1971, and I was being interviewed for a job.

Mary smiled. Her eyes were soft and accepting. It was a testament to her kindness that she didn't laugh. She stirred her latte, espresso swirling to the top. "You come well recommended by Peter," she told me. "He doesn't want to lose you, but he's willing to give you up for Berkeley's first feminist law office."

I was tired of working for men, even though Peter was a fine lawyer and a good person. "I'd really love to work with you," I told her. "Do you think I'd be a good fit?"

"Yes, I do, and Jennie wants you to come on board. Can you start in a couple of weeks?"

I smiled broadly. "Absolutely, I'll tell Peter today." He had hired me on the spot, an untrained legal secretary. When he had asked "How would you rate yourself on a scale of one to ten in terms of organization, one being the least organized," and I had answered "Ten," the job was mine. After working with him for two years, I had become accustomed to an office of male lawyers. Nevertheless, I missed being around women.

I had never worked for a woman. If I were to be honest about it, I'd admit that I had doubts about women's competence as leaders. As I began to realize that I had been molded by the patriarchal views of my upbringing, my attitude changed. I took the job.

In our new office, I sat at the front desk, answered four phone lines like Lily Tomlin in "Nine to Five," greeted clients in the waiting area and, listening to Mary and Jennie's dictation while plugged into a Dictaphone, typed the correspondence and pleadings on a red electric typewriter. I always made three carbon paper copies; Xerox copies were considered a splurge.

Most of our clients were women. The firm did family law, as well as cases related to landlords and tenants, criminal law, personal injury, prison law, and a variety of interesting cases that came our way. We hired women to do repairs, maintenance, plumbing and carpentry work, as well as to be expert witnesses and personal investigators. Whatever we needed done, there was a woman qualified to do it. I began to see that women could do anything.

It was by professional osmosis that I evolved into a feminist who believed I could find my way in the world without a man in charge. The Black Power movement had paved the way for my own growth and empowerment as a woman. Equality and self-determination took on new meaning. I had found a community of women that was changing history, and I felt like I belonged.

It was during this time that I began to think about healing and reclaiming the deep connection I felt with Gerry. It had been three years since his death, and the Unitarian Universalist church in San Francisco became my Sunday ritual. When the congregation sang hymns from my childhood, I wept and felt uplifted. Reverend Harry Schoefield gave talks on heroes of the time, men like Martin Luther King, Huey Newton, Carl Jung, and Milton Erikson. I was inspired in a way I never experienced as a child, a time when the Presbyterian minister's Bible-based sermons put my father to sleep.

This period of my life coincided with my first experience with psychotherapy. I followed this with a Gestalt Therapy group and, eventually, a Bioenergetics group, where I discovered the interplay between mind and body. Three years later, I stopped therapy and joined a women's support group. It was there that I heard about the Berkeley Women's Health Collective, an all-women-run medical clinic. I was curious, but my boyfriend Charlie, a stubborn redhead musician and computer whiz, was suspicious. *Run by only women?* I went anyway.

The collective was in a one-story modern building on Ellsworth Street, just two blocks from the law office. The waiting room was furnished with unmatched fifties sofas and chairs, and the well-equipped exam rooms fanned out on either side of the central hallway. I began to volunteer one evening each week. All volunteers were required to attend the consciousness-raising group. My group of ten women read "Our Bodies Ourselves" and talked intimately about all aspects of our health, as well as our feelings about being women. Any shyness I felt in the beginning quickly disappeared. We learned to insert a speculum into ourselves, and sat in a circle with mirrors and flashlights looking at our vaginas. We talked about our sexual experiences and our orgasms. I felt liberated. I threw out the douche bag my mother had taught me to use, and with it went those memories of being told that "down there" could smell fishy if I didn't keep it flushed out.

We talked about reclaiming our bodies from the male experts and learning how to care for ourselves.

My mother had been a positive role model when it came to being informed about personal health. Her illness qualified her to participate in a research program with yearly inpatient follow-ups, which provided the latest treatments. She was an ideal patient and was articulate about all aspects of her care. Her father was a doctor, so discussions about medical care came easily to her.

While my mother coped heroically with her illness and lived a relatively normal life, she rarely talked about the emotional pain it caused her. She never had ongoing counseling, so many of the psychological issues of illness were avoided. Over the years, when she confided in me, I listened, always feeling sad and helpless, yet determined to ease her pain by hearing her out.

After a time, I became interested in mental health and began to volunteer in the collective's counseling section. A psychologist trained us to assess for depression and suicide. We learned the basic skills of listening and feedback, the most important being empathy, and how to reflect back what we heard by using "I" statements. These tools were important to me, a young woman beginning to feel her power, but not wanting to abuse it. Within a year, I decided to get a masters degree in counseling psychology.

My boyfriend Charlie and I moved in together and shared a life for the next seven years. During that time, both of us completed graduate programs and began our careers. I started a private counseling practice and he started a computer software business. We married in the early eighties, bought a house, and threw out our birth control. I was thirty-seven and no longer haunted by fears of abandonment. Charlie was steady and reliable and I knew he'd be a good father. What was even more important was that I trusted myself. I knew I was on solid ground and believed I could do anything I put my mind to.

PART TWO

1985-1989

TRANSFORMNG

I was traveling alone on a retreat to Tassajara Zen Center, nestled in a mountain valley near the Ventana Wilderness in northern California. This was a training monastery, opened to the public in the summer. I had been here before and planned to immerse myself in meditation, float mindlessly in the Tassajara Creek, and enjoy the natural sauna that arose from the creek and flowed into an ancient steam hut. My hope was to let go of my worry.

When the van reached the top of the mountain, I was feeling anxious. I decided to place my confidence in the driver, a man with steady blue eyes, a gleaming shaved head, and sure hands that dwarfed the steering wheel. I told myself he would negotiate the descent with ease.

For much of my life worry had been my talisman, so deeply ingrained was my mother's refrain: "The things I worry about never happen." I believed that preparing myself for the worst warded off disaster. I had begun to question that belief. The habitual state of worry was robbing me of the joy I desired. Daily meditation had become a comforting balm, and with time I had grown a tougher skin and a more courageous spirit. Now I was wondering if I could simply relax and trust myself to deal with whatever presented itself. It was 1985 and I had just turned forty. What harm could befall me at this peaceful retreat?

"Rattlesnakes," I heard the driver say. "They live among us, so be mindful not to step on one."

Clearly, these reclusive reptiles were not friendly to intruders, which included me.

I conversed quietly with the driver, the two other riders silent. "When I was six," I told him, "my father taught me to ride a horse by reminding me to befriend the huge creature, and to cherish the deep bond that comes from working together. Do you think rattlesnakes respond to the learned fear we have of them?"

He was quiet for a moment and then began to speak. "I heard of such an incident. As the story goes, one warm day, after a lengthy meditation period, a group of monks extended their walking meditation to the courtyard, where they came upon the four-year-old daughter of one of the residents. She was playing with a rattlesnake. The monks, as if one body, formed a circle around the child and the snake and stood there silently, their minds and hearts embracing the girl and her playmate. They smiled in case the child noticed them and became fearful, but she was accustomed to their black-robed presence. Eventually the rattlesnake slipped away and the girl ran off to find her friends."

I was struck by the power of his story as we drove down the mountain to the retreat center below. I felt safe in the car, with him at the wheel.

That evening, I walked to the creek, shed my clothes, and entered the dark water. The steam hut, a moss-covered sanctuary, beckoned me as I swam to its perch on the rocks downstream. I climbed up the two stone steps, and entered the wooden structure, familiar from prior visits. I felt the excitement of returning to a beloved place. It was lit only by the moonlight that shone through foggy corrugated plastic. The smell of sulfur merged with steam rising between the floorboards from the hot spring below, welcoming me with a primitive earthy odor that I had come to associate with healing waters.

"Hello?" I whispered, and was greeted with only an echo. I cherished the solitude as I closed the heavy door, leaving everything I knew behind. A deep silence permeated my mind and the enclosure magnified the damp heat, loosening my neck muscles, and assuring me of the relaxation I sought.

When my eyes got used to the dark, I made out a bench along one side and stretched out on it, feeling its slippery wetness beneath me. My breath deepened, and I entered a dream-like state. A clicking sound began to fill my ears, gradually growing louder, like a cicada or maybe a cricket. I let the sound glide down my body, enlivening my senses. Soon silence returned.

As I lay there, something touched my thigh. It slithered up my belly to rest between my breasts, and then curled around itself. In a deep state of calm, I looked through the mist to face unblinking eyes staring from an elegant triangular head. It rested on my chest as if awaiting a response. I recognized that it was a rattlesnake, yet, oddly, I was not afraid. In fact, I surprised myself by welcoming its presence, sensing it as a spiritual teacher, wondering what it came to tell me. For several minutes we remained connected this way, silently at ease.

Then, as quickly as it came, it slithered away, leaving in its wake a tissue-like replica of itself, a skin outgrown and no longer of service to its expanding body. The serpent didn't look back as it disappeared through a crack under the doorway leading to the icy water below.

I was aware of its absence, a weightlessness where it had been, and I knew that a change had occurred in me. I forgot where I was for a moment, but was pulled back by the sound of my breath. A ray of moonlight caught a luminous vapor arising from my body, an aura that hovered above me, until it slowly disappeared, and left me feeling emotionally and spiritually uplifted. A new clarity of purpose propelled me, and I arose from the bench. Pressing against the heavy door, I exited the chamber and slipped into the water, not knowing what was ahead, and yet open to whatever came my way.

DARKNESS

Charlie and I both felt we had failed in our quest to become parents, despite our willingness to do almost anything to have a baby who was biologically ours. It was 1986 and we had both turned forty-one. Charlie said he felt helpless, while I became more driven. We had joined four other couples in a group organized by RESOLVE, a national organization that offered both information on infertility and an ongoing support group to encourage members to move toward resolution. One couple had given up on pregnancy and decided to foster an older child as a trial run on parenting. Another couple had been told that the husband's sperm were slow swimmers, thus "male motility" was the culprit. A third couple got pregnant just when they decided to adopt. The remaining couple's concerns were similar to ours. The other woman and I had undergone surgeries to clear any blockage in the uterus or the fallopian tubes, taken medication to increase egg production and been instructed on how to maximize conception during sex. Still, there were no pregnancies. Charlie and I considered our options and had finally come up with a plan, which we intended to share with the group.

It was time to leave for our Sunday night RESOLVE meeting. I picked up my mahogany fertility goddess, found months earlier at the Berkeley Flea Market. She was displayed on a bright African cloth with a collection of other ten-inch busts, all uniquely carved. I was taken by her full lips, elongated face and narrowed eyes. Her hair was braided and wrapped around a head held high on broad shoulders. The elderly African saleswoman said that she had been carved in Nigeria, and she advised me to follow the ancient tradition of naming her, placing her on an altar, and confiding my deepest fears and longings to her. She said that if I prayed to the ancient mother to bring my child to me, my life would transform in unimaginable ways. I didn't question her, believing her from the moment she spoke. I was drawn to the woman's black eyes, which appeared both bottomless and light-filled. I felt a bolt of energy run through me as I listened to her.

I named the goddess Darkness, reminding me of the fertile place in my psyche where mysteries reside and transform. Her altar was an oak table that ran the width of an east-facing window in our dining alcove, where the first rays of morning light created an amber glow. A red velvet cloth was laid out with Darkness as the centerpiece. She was flanked by a glass vase of ferns and my mother's silver bowl filled with pomegranates.

Each morning before Charlie awakened, I stood in front of the altar, palms together, expressing myself in a prayerful chant. *I am grieving, I can't conceive. Help me find a way.* I was haunted by a belief that I was *barren*, a word that arose in my psyche when I was fourteen, after I'd confessed to a friend my fear that I would never have a child. I also carried a belief that I was not creative. *Bring light to the darkness. Lead me to my child. Show me the way.* I experienced a feeling of relief, a sense of possibility, and a visceral longing to connect with my child.

We arrived at the meeting, and I was unusually hopeful as we entered the living room of the host couple. I had tucked Darkness under my shawl, holding her near my heart, which warmed at her closeness, and took my place by Charlie in the circle. The check-in began with each couple sharing their good or bad news of the past week. I waited until last, then I pulled Darkness out from under my shawl and introduced her by name, telling how I had found her.

"Charlie and I have decided to adopt," I announced. "I'd like to do an impromptu ritual to initiate Darkness on her journey to find our child. Is everyone willing to help me?" I wondered if people might laugh. We hadn't done anything other than talk in the group.

There were nods and smiles around the circle. Spontaneously, the host stood up and placed a candle on the table. "Let there be fire for illumination and transformation," she said as she lit the candle. I hadn't known I was holding my breath until I exhaled. I felt the comfort of being understood.

Our host's husband stood up and poured water into a small bowl, placing it with the candle. "Let there be water for easy passage."

Getting the hang of it, the couple beside them pulled a fern branch from a flower arrangement and waved it over the table in wide arcs, then placed it on what had now become an altar. "Let there be wind," the husband said, "that this child may take flight on its journey home." I was thrilled at the sense of community and the creative thoughts that were being expressed.

Charlie stood up and took a pebble from a nearby planter. "Let there be earth where the seed may thrive."

I stood and lifted Darkness with outstretched arms. I felt strong and capable. "I name you Darkness, and honor your connection with our child. We wait with open hearts for the arrival of that being." A surge of heat ran down my legs as I gently passed her on to the next person, who added a few words, as did all the others, until she was returned to me. I kissed her forehead and placed her on the altar.

We stood silently in a circle. I felt awed by our connection as I gripped the hands of those on either side of me, at the same time staring at the sacred goddess who had inspired me when traditional medicine could not.

Charlie wept openly and the men embraced him. The group continued as usual, but it was a quiet evening. I allowed my hopes to soar.

One month later we boarded a plane for Hawaii to celebrate our decision, my forty-second birthday and our ten-year anniversary.

INTUITIVELY SPEAKING

She squinted and peered from behind silver-dollar-sized lenses. "What are the three branches of our government?" she asked. Her badge said "Marla, Cognitive Testing," and it was her job to evaluate me. It was Spring 1987.

I knew this test was important to my completing the rehab program. At forty-two, I needed to prove the strength of my memory, yet my mind's eye was staring at a blank screen. Six weeks post brain surgery, and I had been assigned to out-patient rehab. I said nothing, and then I began to panic.

While on vacation in Hawaii to celebrate our decision to pursue adoption— after three long and painful years of infertility treatment—I had become ill. Charlie had taken me to the emergency room of the local hospital, where I was told that I had either a massive tumor and three months to live, or it was a brain abscess that would require surgery and perhaps three months of recovery. I chose to believe it was the latter, as death was not an option at forty-two. It proved to be the abscess, a complication apparently caused by fertility drugs. The neurologist assured me that, with rehabilitation, I'd return to normal.

So here I was, confronted by Marla, and taking a deep breath as I waited for the terror to pass. Instead, my chest tightened and tears spilled from my eyes as I gasped for air. I was alone at the edge of a vast ocean, unsure of what to do next.

Marla out-waited me.

Suddenly, I saw my father's face, his thumbs and index fingers forming a triangle. The words tumbled out of my mouth. "Executive, judicial, and legislative."

"Good. And what are they for?"

Daddy smiled and the words came without thought. "Executive is the president, judicial is the courts, and legislative is the Congress and the House." I felt like a ventriloquist's dummy. Who was speaking through me?

Marla nodded. "What are the major political parties and what are their differences?"

I had no idea. Struggling with this, I remembered the trouble I had with Occupational Therapy. "Show me how to boil an egg," the occupational therapist had said, and I picked up the egg, put it in the pan, shell and all, and turned on the heat. "You might want to put some water in the pan," she told me, which caused me to blush deeply and I filled the pan with water. "Actions that were habitual may be forgotten until the neural pathways are revisited. It's completely natural after the trauma to the brain," she added. Always one who learned by my mistakes, I was grateful to discover this trait was still with me. Shortly thereafter I made an omelet.

Daddy's face appeared again and the words "Democrats and Republicans" came.

"And their differences?" she reminded.

This time, the words came quickly. "Democrats are liberal and Republicans are conservative."

"Good. And what does that mean?"

Again Daddy smiled, and without thinking I said, "Democrats want more government control and Republicans want more individual control." *Where did that come from?* I wondered.

I no longer recall the remaining questions, but I do remember that I passed the test for concept retrieval and was forwarded to Speech Therapy, where the focus was to be on word retrieval. I remember thinking how Daddy always believed I would be a writer, but at this point it seemed unlikely.

Connie, a twentyish girl, blond hair in a high ponytail, lips and fingernails painted cotton-candy pink, smiled enthusiastically, revealing large white teeth. "Let's get started with some lists. How many names of cars can you tell me?"

Blank. I waited for Daddy, but he was AWOL. "Honda," I finally said, as my grey Accord popped into view. The only new car I had ever owned. I loved that car.

"Excellent!" she chirped. "Now imagine yourself with nothing to do, riding around town with friends, naming cars."

First of all, I hadn't simply ridden around since high school, and even then we certainly weren't naming cars. Who was this person? I couldn't do this. "I can't remember any more," I admitted, wondering how I would endure the three months until this was over. Wondering if it would ever be over.

"No problem," she said. "Let's try baseball teams."

I couldn't think of any baseball teams, and I finally confessed as much, followed by, "What's the fucking point of this? I don't watch cars and I don't watch baseball." Though I imagined she had heard this language before, she rolled her eyes and muttered "Whatever." I didn't like feeling incompetent, and I admit I may have been snappy.

After our allotted sessions, Connie cheerfully signed off my chart and referred me to the hospital psychologist, apparently to cure my foul mouth before they discharged me.

Dr. DeWees had graying hair, held loosely in place by tortoise combs with silver inlay. She was kind and didn't ask me to perform. I told her of my failure to list cars and baseball teams. I wondered why they didn't ask for lists of people I loved or feelings that expressed who I was.

She listened intently and then responded, "Words are for more than lists; they are the expression of your thoughts and feelings. Since your left brain is still recovering from the surgery, you may need to rely more on your intuition for a while. That functions from the right side of your brain."

Intuition was not in my vocabulary. In my Midwestern conservative background, intuition was neither valued nor recognized. *Reason* was the ideal. As a child, though words came easily to me, my verbal expressions weren't based on reason. They were shaped by my observations and feelings, which I trusted, and which came with an immediacy that seemed to confuse others. I didn't have a name for it then, but I see now that I was functioning from intuition. Eventually, as my peers became intellectually competitive, I felt pressured to justify any opinion I expressed. I knew *what* I thought, but not always *why* I thought it. I was often at a loss to explain myself, which left me doubting my intelligence. I learned to keep my ideas to myself.

I told Dr. DeWees about my dream of being a mother, and my disappointment that in my current state I wasn't up to the task. "I'm just not mother material," I concluded.

"You'll be a fine mother," she said. "Mothering is intuitive. You'll know what to do." Her reassurance and wisdom didn't penetrate my doubt. She smiled and continued. "It's hard to trust yourself now, but that will come." I felt a glimmer of hope, a feeling that I held in abeyance.

After a few meetings, Dr. DeWees said I no longer needed therapy. She signed off on my chart and I was discharged from rehab. I was still unable to list cars or baseball teams, but that had dropped to the bottom on my *to-do* list as I got my priorities in order.

It was months before I was able to get my husband back on the adoption track, and in time we hired an attorney specializing in private adoptions. She came up with a list of hundreds of prospects, and we crafted a heartfelt letter to potential birth mothers. We attached our smiling self-portraits and dropped boxes of envelopes into the mailbox. Time passed and replies trickled in, most unsuitable, others ruled out after the initial phone call.

One Indian summer day in 1988, I entered Joe Bynes Unique Shoes in Berkeley. Joe could design and make any shoe that his customers wanted. He was a gifted artist.

"How's that baby coming?" he asked, as he packaged my new boots and took my money. "Find one yet?"

"Not yet," I said, "but I'm trying to keep the faith."

"Are you adopting?" came a melodic voice behind me. I turned and saw a woman of undetermined age, her soft cinnamon-hued face open and welcoming. She was dressed in a green and black African tunic and an emerald turban was wrapped around her head, the color mirroring her intense eyes.

"Yes," I said, a bit taken aback, but captivated by her voice.

"If you have a few minutes," she said, "I could help you in your search."

Joe nodded and gave the thumbs-up.

"Thank you, I'd like that," I found myself saying, surprised at how at ease I felt. We walked to a quiet corner of the shop and sat.

She didn't waste any time. "Can you describe what your baby looks like?"

This is when I realized that I had been visualizing my daughter for months. "She has honey-blonde hair, green eyes, and a strong Midwestern body."

"That's wonderful," she said. "Would you be willing to close your eyes and listen for a while?"

I nodded. Eyes closed, I focused on her voice. I was reassured that she was more than a Berkeley weirdo.

"Put your hand on your heart and feel your heartbeat as I talk," she instructed. "Imagine the birthmother who is looking for you; see her pregnant belly and your daughter inside, waiting to be born."

In my mind emerged a small circle with a flame in the middle. The circle transformed into a woman pacing and holding her belly. The flame became a fetus that illuminated her womb, its form rhythmically throbbing in sync with my heartbeat. A soft tenderness overcame me, and I felt as if I were floating in the gentle tide of an ocean.

"Feel the directness of the mother's gaze as she searches to find you," said the woman. "See yourself as the perfect mother, in the perfect circumstance to receive this child. Now imagine yourself meeting and talking with the woman in person or by phone."

I saw myself at home, on the phone, the massive redwood standing sentinel outside my window, and swaying in the wind, sounding a steady ahhhh sound, like a midwife coaching me to exhale.

"Hold these images in your heart," said this stranger, "and call them up whenever you are afraid. They will bring your daughter to you."

I had been advised by an infertility specialist years ago to visualize being pregnant. I found this illusive. I tried hard to do it but no images came to my mind. The best I could do was draw a picture of my ovaries and my uterus, and then show my husband's sperm swimming up the fallopian tubes to fertilize my eggs. I remained infertile, but something was changing. This time, the images were coming to me spontaneously.

I opened my eyes and saw the woman walking out the door, her caftan billowing in the breeze. I asked Joe who she was and learned that she was Celeste.

"An old soul," he told me. "She's been coming here for years. Trust her, she knows what she's talking about."

I walked out in a daze, pondering what had just happened.

Within a week, we received a call from Carly. She had chosen our letter from more than the forty she had received.

"I just knew," she said. "When I read your letter, I knew I wanted you to be my baby's mother."

I felt an immediate connection with this woman, and after a brief conversation, I, too, knew that she was the one, a certainty not arrived at by logic or reason, but by intuition. It was years later that I understood how Dr. DeWees and Celeste had helped me to understand that listening to my instincts was as valuable as the straight lines of linear thought.

My green-eyed, blonde and athletic daughter was born in Carly's hometown of Garden City, Kansas, and we adopted her at birth. This event took place exactly two years to the day of my brain surgery.

GREEN BOUGH IN MY HEART

It was February 14, 1989, my forty-fourth Valentine's Day. Breakfast on silver tray was only a token when compared to the gift in our bed. Lulu, our newborn daughter, lay between Charlie and me. Born eleven days earlier, she was the center of our lives. Her eyes, the jade of deep tropical water, gazed with eager curiosity as we played finger and toe games and made up silly songs.

> *Lulu on the lily pad, floating in the pond*
> *Watching all the koi fish, going round and round*
> *Along came the raccoons looking for a snack*
> *But this beaming baby Buddha sent them running*
> *for their back.*

I thought back to Lulu's first home, only ten days ago, in Garden City, Kansas, a windowless hotel room with recessed lighting behind glass panels, creating the illusion of sky. With baby bottles in the cooler and an electric water pot to heat them, we had everything we needed. We fed her when she was hungry, and when she slept, we tucked her into the nest of soft blankets lining the mahogany drawer we'd removed from the dresser. Charlie sang "You Are My Sunshine" and I cooed in high trills and murmured words of love.

Carly, the birthmother, had invited us to the birth. We arrived early in the morning, but Lulu had already made her appearance. There was a welcoming ceremony, so we had to wait, while Carly and her mother cuddled with Lulu. Carly's husband Ron was at work, and we called him and he gave us his blessing.

As I watched Carly with Lulu, I was dizzy with anticipation. I remembered my friend Glorinda, an adoption social worker, reminding me to let Carly take her time. "You want her to choose the moment to relinquish her baby," she told me, "and not feel pressured." Glorinda reminded me that this would allow her to separate at her pace, which was crucial. The last thing that I wanted was for Carly to change her mind.

And so I restrained myself, aching arms at my side, working hard to swallow the words "May I hold her for just a minute?"

I can't recall how I felt when Carly handed Lulu to me, her new mother. Was it rapture? Amazement? It was a blur of emotions.

As Charlie quickly guided me to our car, I was consumed by the baby's fresh fragrance and the weight of her nine pounds cradled in my arms. I gazed at my daughter and silently vowed I would protect her with my life. As soon as the car started, she fell asleep. Holding her, I began to memorize her features: alabaster skin, wisps of blonde eyebrows, cheeks like pillows, a rosebud nose, and perfect heart-shaped lips.

Charlie drove to the hotel where we stayed for three days. There was a legal requirement that we give Carly that length of time to change her mind. During those days I was so transfixed by Lulu's presence that I never left the room. Charlie's only forays away from his new family included a local Chinese take-out for Hot and Sour soup and fortune cookies. On three occasions, I received the same fortune. *If you keep a green bough in your heart, the singing bird will come.*

When the waiting period came to an end and there was, to our relief, no word from Carly, we flew back to California. Carly had agreed we would have no contact until Lulu was eighteen. Only then could Lulu decide if she wanted to reconnect.

We settled into our new routine of making formula, changing diapers, and feeding our baby. Charlie and I were a good team, sharing in everything and loving our new roles. Lulu also settled in, adapting to her new life. She ate and slept with ease. And when she gazed into my eyes I knew that I had never been happier or more at peace.

On that first Valentine's Day together, Charlie separated himself from us, took the empty bottle and crawled out of bed. He returned shortly with a pile of mail. I sorted through the envelopes and recognized the return address of a lawyer in Kansas City. I ripped it open and felt dread when I saw that it was from an attorney representing Richey, "the birth father." This was when we discovered that Lulu's biological father was not Carly's husband, and that this man was requesting custody. For a moment I felt as though my heart had flat-lined.

"I was afraid something like this would happen," Charlie said. His emergency call to our lawyer was returned promptly.

The next step was a phone appointment with a specialist in adoption custody, who outlined a strategy that included delaying the hearing for as long and possible. This would strengthen our argument that Lulu was bonded to me, and that any change of custody would not be in her interest.

As the days progressed, I wondered if Carly and this man were working together. As much as rage boiled through me, I was determined to remain emotionally balanced, and I wondered if fate had prepared me for this moment. I knew that our Lulu was receptive to everything around her and I feared she would resonate to my turmoil. I knew all too well how children take on the tension around them, having suffered from my childhood wish to save my mother from illness and the pressure I felt to adapt to her emotional needs. I understood this about myself, and how my mother's health penetrated and shaped my life. But had it groomed me for the kind of selfless detachment required in this situation, when faced with losing my child?

That Lulu and I got through this period unscathed seems, at times, like a miracle. At other times, I see clearly that inside the human psyche is a well of unconditional love and a longing to express it. I had touched that well.

Each time that rage and fear returned, I stepped onto our deck and bowed before the ancient redwood tree, a towering reminder of strength, its green branches silhouetted against the sky. As I prayed, I asked that this majestic tree impress itself on my psyche and release me from my negative emotions.

Paternity tests proved Richey to be the father; a court date was scheduled. During the eight weeks before the hearing, we held Lulu close, imprinting her entire being on ourselves, and we tried to go about our lives. We refused to let this potential nightmare rob us of the joy of being a family. We had what we wanted, and we intended to do everything possible to keep it.

At the hearing, I had my first look at Lulu's father. He was tall and thin, nice enough looking, but impossible to read. During the proceedings, he made no contact with Carly who was seated alone in the front row yet he often looked at me, smiling. During a break, Carly asked if we could go somewhere private.

We stood together in the empty restroom, her words echoing off white tile walls and floor. "It was an affair," she explained. "I didn't tell him that he was the father, and I didn't tell my husband, either." She went on to explain that, when she finally told her husband, he couldn't accept it. "He wanted to separate" she said, "but Richey got wind of this and told me he wanted to marry me and raise the baby. I told him no, so he got a lawyer."

Carly was tearful as she recounted this, but she was also direct, her look steady and sure as she confessed. "I still want you and Charlie to raise Lulu," she said. She had told Richey's lawyer the same, and would repeat this to the judge. When she added, "Please don't worry, I will be fine," her eyes were pleading, as if trying to connect with mine. Hoping, it seemed, for reassurance.

Still frightened, I could offer only a frozen smile. Did I believe her? I'm not sure. I stammered, "Thanks for telling me," and rushed back to the courtroom. I hoped this was important evidence, and I reported the conversation to my lawyer.

The hearing was brief, the judge setting another date for eight weeks later. In the meantime, I was to meet with a bonding psychologist who would evaluate my relationship with Lulu and report back to the judge. Another eight weeks seemed unendurable, but again we got through it, savoring every minute with our Lulu.

When I went to the appointment I had to fight a nagging doubt that I might fail to prove myself. Lulu was nearly four and a half months now, and it was inconceivable that she would be taken away. We were escorted into a playroom where the psychologist, an older, grey-haired woman with a tight smile, asked me several questions. Did I have younger siblings? *No.* Was my husband supportive? *Yes.* Did I think that forty-four was too old to have an infant? *No.* With each response I hoped that I was supporting my case. She told me to put Lulu down on the playroom floor and walk away. I was uncomfortable doing this, but followed her directions, placing Lulu on her tummy.

My daughter immediately lifted her head and began to cry. Before I could pick her up, the doctor told me to stay where I was and encourage Lulu to come to me. I wanted to win this game so I knelt down, clapped my hands and sang our favorite song about Lulu on the lily pad. As I sang, I felt myself grinning awkwardly, my voice catching in my throat.

At first, Lulu looked surprised, and my heart sank, but soon she was see-sawing along, what Charlie and I called her rocking horse move and she came toward me at full speed. When she arrived at my knees, I scooped her up and held her to my chest, laughing triumphantly into her joyous face. The doctor nodded, and said, "She has certainly bonded." With that she stood, shook my hand, and told me we were free to go.

Lulu and I sailed out the door, my relief so great I felt as if I could levitate. Peruvian lilies with coral faces shone in the brilliant sun, and I was elated. A sense of hope permeated my heart. I took Lulu's hand and placed it on my chest, so grateful for her presence in my life.

The judge awarded us custody. That same day, I stood on the deck with Lulu in my arms, thinking of my own mother. I had been her third child. When she had fallen ill, I remember wondering if having me had been too much for her. I lived for years with that concern, making me fearful that I overwhelmed others. Perhaps this was why I tended to diminish myself and my creativity.

Holding my daughter, I vowed that Lulu would always know she was loved, accepted and cherished exactly as she was.

We both looked out at the giant redwood, and Lulu began to coo. I recalled the fortune cookie that promised *If you keep a green bough in your heart the singing bird will come.* I gazed down at my daughter and laughed. Here, in my arms, was my singing bird.

PART THREE

1995-2007

SHOW OF SUPPORT

"You probably should remove your dangly earrings, someone might try to snatch them," whispered my new supervisor while giving me a tour of the psychiatric hospital.

It was April of 1995, and I was recovering from the unraveling of my marriage and the divorce that followed. I had been working extra hours in several hospital emergency rooms, assessing people for transfer to psychiatric facilities. Now here I was, beginning a new job, walking the wards where I had sent those same people. This was my first time inside a psychiatric hospital and I was impressed by the modern layout, though I couldn't help but to think of Jack Nicholson and Nurse Ratchett.

A squat woman caught my eye and smiled. "Can you get me out of here?" she asked, pushing a mass of disheveled hair from her eyes. "I don't want to hurt nobody." In her forties, the standard-issue green pajamas clung to her thick body.

"I'm Ellen," I responded. "How are you today?"

She eyed me suspiciously. "Why are you so friendly?"

A young man was suddenly at the woman's side and my supervisor nowhere to be seen. "Irma, who are you talking to?" he said gently. I noticed his badge: *Troy, Mental Health Worker.*

Irma smiled and inched closer to me. "This is Ellen; she's a friend of mine."

Troy nodded. "Hi, Ellen, I'm Irma's contact person today." He turned to the woman. "Did you tell Ellen why you're here?"

"I hit a man at my Board and Care because he was bothering me," she admitted.

Troy's chuckle was almost inaudible. He smiled warmly and continued, "And did you tell Ellen what led up to that?"

"I was off my meds. I ran out." Wide-eyed, she raised her eyebrows, waggling her head as if claiming innocence.

"And you didn't call your case manager, right?" urged Troy. "People usually call their case managers when they need more meds." He looked at me before adding, "Leland always helps when you call him."

"So I was high," said Irma. "So what? Just let me out of here. Ellen, can you get me out?"

I knew not to get involved. "I don't think that's up to me," I told her. "Maybe once your meds kick in you'll be in a better position."

"Screw you, bitch," Irma spat, then turned on her heels and walked away.

Troy crossed his arms and stood with legs apart, a towering figure at over six feet. As he spoke, he kept his eyes on Irma. "Is this your first day?"

He seemed friendly. Was I being sized up? "Pretty obvious, huh?" I countered.

"No, not at all," he smiled, and went on to explain how Irma runs out of meds, gets high on cocaine to stop the voices, gets in trouble with the police, and then ends up back in this facility.

"You've probably heard that we're a revolving door, but I think the regulars consider us family," he explained. "We know them, we know their history, and we don't judge them. We give them meds, limits, TLC, and when they're ready, we kick them out. That is, if they haven't already gotten a judge to release them."

"Are there any violent patients?" I asked, beginning to wonder if I'd be killed here. I was working full time because I had primary custody of my six-year-old daughter. This was a union job with a good salary and excellent benefits, but I needed to be safe and go home at night. .

"A few can become violent," said Troy, "but we talk them down, if possible. Otherwise, we put them in a time-out in their room. If they refuse that, we go for the staff *show of support* and take them to the restraint room. Old school, we called it *show of force*, but now they sugar-coat it and call it *show of support*."

I didn't have a clue about these things, and his expression told me that he sensed this. Was I expected to participate in restraining a patient without being trained? "Don't worry," he said. "You're a social worker, right?"

I nodded.

"We've got your back. It's Mental Health Workers and Nursing's job to maintain the peace. You get to calm down the families and the care providers."

I looked around and saw patients sitting at tables and talking intently with staff. Others sat alone, tapping their toes as Nina Simone sang "Feeling Good" on the boom box.

"What's your secret?" I asked.

Troy thought about this for a moment, and then said, "Respect. Bottom line: if they feel your respect, even if they're psychotic, most will eventually talk to you. That's how you get to know them, and how you let them see that you can help them, if they're willing to do their part."

An image flashed in my mind of my father banging on my locked bedroom door when I was twenty. I had walked away from an argument about something minor, and when he demanded that I unlock the door, I refused. He left, but soon returned with a screwdriver. As he worked on the doorknob, he yelled, "Come out now!" I had been going to college and living in the apartment in the back of my parents' house, but I usually came and went without incident. My mother was gone that day, in the hospital for her yearly check-up, evoking my fears of a re-activation of her illness. She would have calmed Daddy down, but I could not. Instead, I unlocked the door and screamed in his face, "Leave me alone, I hate you!" He shook me and said I was acting crazy. So I shut down and backed off, afraid he might be right.

As if in segue to my fantasy, I heard a female voice yelling, "Leave me alone or you'll regret it." Troy was standing quietly while talking to Irma, who had her fists clenched and knees slightly bent as she danced from foot to foot like a boxer in the ring. "Come and get it!" she shouted, her eyes flashing and her face contorted.

"You can take a time-out in your room," said Troy, his voice gentle, yet firm. "And take your meds; you'll feel better."

Irma lunged at him. Troy backed away, prepared for what was coming. Suddenly, six staff members appeared, walking slowly, voices calm, all suggesting a time-out. I knew to help herd the other patients into the TV room, explaining that Irma would be fine with her meds and a time-out. And then I watched from a safe distance.

It was like a choreographed dance in slow motion, with a soundtrack of soothing murmurs. Except for Irma's voice, which became thunderous. Her eyes froze in a startled stare. Suddenly, Troy took her by one arm; a nurse took her by the other, with two more staff in front and three in back. They surrounded Irma like a sixties group hug about to unfold. But she needed more than a hug.

I followed as they led Irma to Room A-2. It was a smaller, windowless version of the patient rooms, with one bare bed fitted with leather restraints for hands, feet, and waist. Irma was almost docile as she sat on the bed. No restraints were used. She was given emergency medication, then the door was closed and locked.

I peeked into the small window at the top of the door and watched. She was sitting quietly on the bed. Troy checked on her fifteen minutes later and she announced that she wouldn't yell or threaten anyone, so he agreed to let her out.

Later, I would discover that life didn't always run this smoothly on the psych ward. There were complaints by family members, demands by patients' rights advocates, everyone insisting that patients were being treated unfairly, even punitively. Looking back, I cannot recall witnessing one incident of patient abuse, but it did exist, usually when inexperienced staff intervened at the wrong time.

As my tour was coming to an end, Troy said, "So you got to see a show of force on your first day. Trial by fire."

"You guys were amazing," I told him. "She really responded to your sense of calm. I would call it a show of support. How do you do it?"

"Teamwork," he told me. "We know from experience that if we react, it will only frighten her more."

I scanned the room and crossed my arms, breathing shallowly at the scent of meatloaf and overcooked vegetables that had just arrived on a cart. "She didn't seem frightened to me, she seemed pissed."

"The anger is a cover," he explained as he eyed a patient pacing the floor. "Her voices probably told her we were going to hurt her, so she was protecting herself. She hasn't stabilized on her meds yet. She's only been here two days."

Troy would become one of my best teachers in the fifteen years I worked with him. I never heard him raise his voice, nor fail to get patients talking about themselves. Being handsome didn't hurt, but I think it was more his manner. He had a directness that patients trusted, and a curiosity about who they were. He expected the best from them, and he expected them to be accountable. That drew people to him. During my career, I learned that most people want to free themselves from their destructive behavior.

Changing my own behavior hadn't always been so easy. For as long as I could remember, I had wanted to be able to soothe my father, who struggled, as did I, with an exaggerated fear of losing Mother. The older I got, the more I reacted with anger when I sensed his anxiety, or when he expressed his feelings loudly. It was Mother who could reassure and calm him. She was to Daddy what Troy and his team were to Irma: an island of calm in the face of turbulence. Though I could never play that role with my father, and failed in my marriage to soothe my husband's anger, I did learn, in fifteen years on the psych ward, to work in harmony with my team and to be a balm to myself when my fear of loss began to cloud my judgment. And, like Irma, I learned to ask for help when I needed it, a skill that made my life as a single mother less lonely and more manageable.

MISS PRETTY

Miss Pretty was a blue-eyed demon. An Alaskan Husky, she was known to bite and had been to doggy jail in the past year. She was a fixture inside the iron gate surrounding the yard and the driveway, which I traversed daily outside my apartment. My daughter and I lived in the upper rear flat of a massive red Victorian, and shared a deck with four students who lived in the upper front. Not only was it an apartment I could afford as a single parent, but it was next door to the Zen Center where I practiced meditation. Below us reigned our landlady, Slim, living alone in a multi-room flat filled with mismatched furniture and piles of empty boxes left over from incomplete projects.

Like Miss Pretty, Slim had a quick temper and a sarcasm that often manifested as a poison pen. Scathing epistles, typed in twenty-four point caps appeared intermittently on my door for all to see. In them she found fault with my personality, my tone of voice, my parenting skills, and any planter that I placed on the deck. She was envious that I had a green thumb, while her plants turned brown and were left to die. Though we rarely talked, she disliked the fact that I stayed on, while other tenants, mostly students, left their apartments after a year or two, allowing her to raise the rent. I was protected by rent control, so the rent was raised by one or two percent each year. Over the years, she became more hostile, hissing "Watch out" or "Run" when I walked down the driveway. I looked straight ahead and said nothing, but consulted with the rent board from time to time, to make sure any problem was resolved.

Later, Slim would threaten to evict us and move in a family member, but my long-term tenancy secured my status as a protected class by rent control standards. I loved my Victorian apartment with its large windows, hardwood floors and twelve-foot ceilings, and I had no intention of leaving. I planned to retire and begin a new life as a writer in my cozy apartment.

In my mind, I was an ideal tenant: a quiet minimalist who paid her rent ahead of time, got along with her neighbors, and recycled all her trash. Slim, however, saw it differently. She knew she had control over what was necessary to me: my home and my security. She never failed to remind me that she could snatch it all away, or drive me out by her bad behavior.

As a student of meditation, I sat every day on my cushion and faced the demons of fear and anger evoked by her toxic ways. I focused myself with this meditation poem: *In, out/ deep, slow/ calm, ease/ mind, release /present moment, wonderful moment.* Each time the negative feelings arose, I tried to remember to breathe and affirm that I was more than my emotions. It was a slow process, but I kept at it.

Slim sometimes swore at me as I walked down the driveway, where she stood hosing the lawn, dressed in her sweat pants and faded flannel shirt. Her grey hair and lined face were a testament to her fifty years of woe. Her moods were soon ignored by the neighbors, though Miss Pretty remained at her side, a captive audience. We tenants were holding our collective breath, awaiting Slim's response if Miss Pretty got hit with a second strike, removing her from society for good. In the doggy world, the death penalty prevails.

One spring morning I heard a scream outside the window and ran to my deck overlooking the yard and street below. A sobbing young girl was being pulled down the sidewalk by her mother. I heard Miss Pretty yelping as I saw her tail disappear into Slim's apartment. The door slammed and Slim yelled, "Bad dog, Miss Pretty, bad dog."

Had the inevitable occurred? A call from the next-door neighbor confirmed that her six-year-old niece had been bitten by Miss Pretty. Slim had warned the frightened child that if she told the police, Miss Pretty would be killed. The girl was inconsolable when, at the emergency room, the doctor said he was legally bound to report the attack to Animal Control. The mother immediately wrote a letter to Animal Control asking for a stay, if Slim would put up additional dog-proof fencing around the yard. The case was continued for six months.

Miss Pretty was all Slim had. When I first rented the apartment, my daughter Lulu was six years old. Slim's son Julep had graduated high school that year and had moved out shortly after we'd moved in. He stayed away. That was when Slim got Miss Pretty, saying it was too hard to live alone. Various boyfriends moved in and out, but Miss Pretty always stayed.

Miss Pretty had always been friendly to me, and was particularly fond of Lulu, for whom she would roll on her back, feet in the air, demanding a tummy rub, which Lulu would provide with pleasure. Miss Pretty seemed to consider us family. Having known us since she was a puppy, she never growled or snapped at us, as she did at strangers. And Lulu had a special gift with animals, a fun-loving warmth that brought them to her, seeking love. It was amazing to watch. Miss Pretty would bound up to Lulu as soon as she entered the gate after school, and Lulu would drop her pack in the driveway and wrestle with Miss Pretty, who never bared her teeth. Soon they were chasing the soccer ball that lay idle in the yard, until Miss Pretty plopped down for the tummy rub.

Apparently, Miss Pretty only bit people who reached through the fence to pet her as she sat sunning by the gate. She was very appealing, with ice blue eyes, a long fluffy grey and white coat, and a curved mouth that looked to be perpetually smiling. Slim had posted *Beware of Dog* signs, but they didn't stop most people, especially neighborhood folks. I had heard from a man who had known Slim for years that he was passing the gate when Miss Pretty approached him, wagging her tail. He bent down to her level, pooched his lips in a kiss, and she lunged at his mouth, tearing his lip. That was the first strike, again because the ER had to report. "I almost didn't go, but my lip was torn and blood was everywhere" was how he justified it when Slim stopped speaking to him.

Slim had made a special effort to reconnect with her son Julep. He was committing to his life partner and had invited Slim to drive him down the grassy aisle of his outdoor ceremony in Golden Gate Park. Slim painted her 1964 VW bug mint green, put the top down and filled the back seat with baby pink roses. Julep rode shotgun in the parade that ended at a knoll where his partner awaited. A neighbor who attended reported that something went wrong. Before the reception, Slim jumped in the car and drove off without explanation. I never saw Julep visit his mother after that day, and Slim was left alone with Miss Pretty. I found myself worrying about what would happen if Miss Pretty were put down, and whether there was anything I could do to prevent her demise.

I have never been responsible for anyone's death, but had carried for many years a fear of death for those I loved. A wise therapist helped me to see that my fear was rooted in a sense of responsibility that I had adopted as a child, due to my mother's rare illness. I was only six, yet I wondered if I had caused her to be sick, and if I could prevent further occurrences and potential death by being a better girl. My mother lived into her eighties, and I was finally able to release that guilt. That is, until Miss Pretty evoked that childhood anguish.

After the potential second strike, Miss Pretty and Slim kept a low profile for weeks and eventually reappeared in the yard. Slim greeted me with her usual invectives and left occasional toxic notes on my door. Within a few months, Miss Pretty disappeared. The rumor was that she had committed another crime, though no one knew for sure, and Slim wasn't talking. It remained an unsolved mystery, and in time was forgotten.

Years later, still in the same apartment, I awake at dawn, having dreamed about Miss Pretty. In the dream, she is stretched out on a white velvet bed. With paws serenely raised, she looks like a dog who only wants love, but even in a dream-like state I see all too clearly the harm she can inflict. I see her beautiful silver and black coat shiver as the alcohol swab is placed on her neck. I feel my nose sting as the needle is injected and the sharp medicinal smell permeates the room. Slim stands nearby, stoic, eyes closed, repeating the words *I'm sorry*. I feel compassion for her pain and sense our connection.

Miss Pretty goes quickly; her black lips open in a smile, her white teeth gleaming. When her breath stops, I see her spirit rise like smoke, disappearing into the air. I take a deep breath and find myself in the presence of a warm and embracing energy, and hear myself say *I forgive me*. I feel as if a weight has been lifted and I gratefully release it.

There is the familiar clatter of glass on glass in the recycling bin. Slim is yelling, probably to the homeless woman who collects bottles early on pick-up day, "You box of rocks, that's for paper!" Hearing her voice reminds me of the dream, as well as the compassion I felt for Slim. It's painful to think about the hurt she inflicts on others, and it's unsettling to accept that she may never change. Like Miss Pretty, she is a victim of her animal instincts.

BECOMING

I felt a tug in my heart which spoke familiarity, but I saw only the back of a child and didn't recognize her for a moment. With blonde hair neatly French-braided, my nine-year-old daughter was dressed in a turquoise blouse with matching pants and sandals. She usually wore casual athletic clothes. When she turned to face me I gave her my brightest smile. "Lulu, you're all dressed up!"

She rolled her eyes and gave a slight shake of her head. Her body language spoke clearly and I knew to let it go.

"How do you like Glo's show?" I asked. Lulu had come with her dad and step-mom to her Godmother Glorinda's art show at the Richmond Art Center. Glorinda , treasured by Lulu's dad and me, had made sure we all attended. She liked to bring the family together.

I had left my daughter at school three days earlier. She was sporting her usual athletic pants, t-shirt, and Nikes, her long hair slightly tangled. Now here she was, transformed into a girly-girl, most likely at her stepmother's urging. The woman was nearby. I couldn't see her, but I felt her presence. Our custody schedule specified that Lulu spend Thursday through Saturday nights at her dad's in the Oakland hills, and Sunday through Wednesday nights with me in the Berkeley flats. Her stepmother denied me any phone or physical contact while Lulu was at their home, and referred to herself as Lulu's mother, insisting Lulu do likewise. In all the years that Lulu stayed with them, I never saw the inside of their house.

Once, when my sister was in town, we came at Lulu's invitation to hear her at-home concert, and were told to walk around to the back door, where we were made to stand outside. My daughter and her father serenaded us through the open French doors. When the music was over, Lulu came out, shrugging, as we enthused about her talent as a violinist, and quickly guided us on a tour of her chicken coop, introducing us by name to each of her seven beloved chickens. I often thought it was those chickens who saved Lulu at that house. She poured her love into them, and miraculously managed to adapt. I often worried that she would learn from this woman's poisonous efforts to deny my existence, to simply shut me out of her heart. Or worse yet, that this woman's voice would overpower Lulu's before she learned to hear it and trust it as her own. As Lulu walked us to our car that day, she seemed happy, knowing she would soon be home. The stepmother never showed her face.

So, here we were, at the exhibit, and my little girl wasn't looking so little.

"I like it," she said, gesturing toward the art. "Did you see Glorinda? She's over there."

"I'll go see her now" I smiled, sensing the stepmother's glare. I knew that she couldn't be reasoned with and would take it out on Lulu if we talked too long. I made a quick exit after stealing a hug and whispering "See you at five." I had made a choice years ago to withdraw from the stepmother's maternal power struggle that threatened to put a wedge between Lulu and me, creating enormous stress for my daughter. Though I grieved the loss of contact when we were apart, I reminded myself that a deeper connection, which I lived for, was preserved by my actions. To survive the weekly separations, each morning I went to the Zen Center next to my house, entered the zendo and sat in silence with others. When the gong sounded, we arose and chanted:

> *All my ancient, twisted karma*
> *From beginningless greed, hate and delusion*
> *I now fully avow.*

Descending to our knees, we bowed from the waist, arms outstretched in a posture of surrender and release. My judgments of the stepmother's callousness that burned in my brain were momentarily lifted. Just as the chickens calmed Lulu, the Zen Center provided me with solace, a spiritual practice and community that allowed me to live with a destructive presence in my life, yet not be defined by it.

    I drove home from the art exhibit and wondered if I was depriving Lulu of the self-expression that clothes could provide. Did she enjoy dressing like that, or was she choosing to go along with her stepmother's choices? Lulu had once broken her dad's rule by talking to me about the stepmother. It seems the woman had given Lulu advice on how to choose clothes that would give her a better shape and deal with her "weight problem." What in the world was this woman thinking? I had felt a searing in my gut at not being able to stop this talk. Lulu was a muscular, athletic girl, already perfect and certainly not overweight, and I worried that she was afraid to voice her disagreement. Or maybe she was reluctant to complain to *me* about her wardrobe, which consisted of little more than the casual, athletic clothing she stored in the armoire that served as her closet. Perhaps if she had a real closet, one where she could hang stylish outfits, she'd ask me to French-braid her hair and buy her bright-colored clothes and sandals. I had never remarried and my salary didn't go far. Sometimes I felt guilty that I couldn't afford to provide more for her. Maybe that's why she hadn't asked. Was I failing in my conviction to honor her individuality? Or was I just slipping into doubt?

    I knew the adage about parents wanting more for their children than they had been given, but I was living more modestly than I had while growing up. I consoled myself that I would have a closer bond with my daughter than I had with my mother, from whom I had often felt disconnected. Without knowing it, I had shaped myself to gain her approval, which I had hoped would make us closer. This was the last thing I wanted for my daughter, living her life to please me. Lulu's freedom to be herself was everything to me.

    One day, weeks after Glo's exhibit, on a lunch hour trek to buy cheap gas, I passed by

Thriftown and decided to take a look. Directly inside the front entrance were paintings, ceramics, and books, and a bank of six cashiers waiting to ring up my purchases. The barn-like space was filled with clothes, household items, bedding, knick-knacks, toys, furniture, jewelry, bicycles, and much more, all clustered by category and designated by black and white signs hanging from the ceiling. Many things looked new and the prices were low. I wondered if Lulu might find some clothes she liked here.

I flitted from department to department, giddy with so many affordable items. There was even a high-end women's section where I immediately found a red velvet shirt for seven dollars and a pair of Chico's jeans for five. I grabbed both, forgetting that I had come to shop for Lulu. She had been getting by on hand-me-downs from cousins and gifts from my sister. Thriftown was a step up.

Moving through the Thriftown aisles, I glanced in the mirror at my basic black outfit, the nineties look for middle-aged meditating Berkeley women. I always wore my Zen silver necklace and earrings, and on special occasions threw on a cobalt scarf. Finding a store I could afford allowed me to play with self-expression. I mused how my new red shirt would bring out my strawberry blond hair, and even imagined releasing the ponytail I usually wore. Maybe I could buy brown pants with an orange or yellow top, or even brown shoes. The thought of adding a gold necklace felt almost subversive.

It wasn't long after her new clothing reveal at the arts center that I took Lulu to Thriftown to celebrate her first double-digit birthday. Somewhere in the women's section she blew me a kiss and said, "See you later," heading off to explore. As she disappeared into the forest of clothes under the "Girls" sign, I wondered if she would emerge as the girl I had not recognized, or the girl I knew so well. I feared a moment of truth that would prove *me* to be the mother who was blind to my daughter's efforts to express herself.

Thriftown was, as usual, a mesmerizing experience. Inside that cavernous space, I lose track of time, submerged in a sea of colors and forms. On that day, with Lulu, I felt abundant and hopeful, as if I were about to eat a sumptuous and expensive meal which would satisfy my hunger and not break the bank.

I wasn't surprised when an hour had passed before Lulu tapped me on the shoulder and said, "Mom, I've been in Men's. Those clothes fit me better and I found some really cool stuff." That said, she disappeared. I took a deep breath and exhaled my relief, knowing that she was still my girl.

A few minutes later, I found her in the Men's section, arms loaded with athletic pants, t-shirts and her prize discovery, a lime green Nike running suit with a single white stripe on the pants. As I paid the cashier, Lulu turned to me and said, "Thanks, Mom, for letting me get what I really wanted." I felt a rush of love.

"You're welcome, sweet Lulu. Only you know what's right for you," I said, touching her slightly tangled hair, cherishing this moment and the connection that comes when a child's independence is honored. She, too, was glowing, holding the green suit to her torso and twirling to show it off.

Looking back, it is amazing to see how the clever stepmother unwittingly deepened my bond with my daughter and supported her individuality. By excluding me from contact with her, I saw Lulu with fresh eyes each time she came home, and I took pleasure in nurturing her budding growth and independence, knowing that our connection was secure.

TUMBLEWEED

When I saw the tumbleweed rolling through the parking lot at the outlet mall near Phoenix, I just knew that it was the solution to our holiday tree dilemma. My mind was exhausted from hours on the road, and was suddenly flooded with a vision of this perfect sphere strung with lights and hanging from the twelve-foot ceiling in our living room back in Berkeley. I could just see all the cock-eyed ornaments we had collected or made over the years, dangling gracefully from its orb-like splendor. Our eight-hundred square-foot South Berkeley apartment never looked so fine. I had to have that tumbleweed.

I had recently admitted to myself that there was no way I could continue competing with my ex-husband when it came to holiday traditions. As a single parent, I was tired of poking through the local Delancey Street Christmas tree lot in early December, looking for the tiniest table-top tree, while knowing that my daughter Lulu, now eleven, would soon climb into her dad's BMW for their yearly trek to the forest, where they would chop down a huge evergreen, then decorate it with fragile ornaments, while sipping spiced apple cider and eating cinnamon rolls served on Spode china by Lulu's stepmother.

I had begun to feel that a change was in order. For too long I had forfeited both Christmas and Thanksgiving to Lulu's dad and stepmother, as if their large extended family entitled them to it. I wanted Lulu to have more time with my family, small though it was. When she turned eleven, which was shortly before my fifty-fifth birthday, we decided to make our claim on Thanksgiving weekend. This year it would be spent with my sister Cari, Lulu's favorite aunt, in Tempe, Arizona. My parents were no longer alive and my brother, though nearby, was usually busy, so this was going to be a small, intimate, loving group of family. And while Lulu's dad may have considered it a paltry alternative to their grand affairs, my daughter and I mapped out our road trip with great excitement and were soon on our way.

Sally, our Golden Retriever, reigned from the back seat of our '97 Honda Odyssey, and Lulu set up shop with a TV table and her school books in the furthest back seat. I slipped behind the wheel and took command of the CD collection. Easy. Six hours on the road, a stay in a Motel Six, six more hours of driving. Beatles songs were at the top of my list, so I belted out "Rocky Raccoon" as I barreled down the I-60, smiling at the image of Rocky shooting off the legs of his rival.

When I saw that tumbleweed rolling past, during a pit stop at a McDonald's, I envisioned not only Thanksgiving as becoming uniquely ours, but Christmas as well. Call me greedy, but I wanted to shut down the comparisons in my mind. Yes, we could still celebrate the holiday the second week of December, an arbitrary date that, as a Buddhist, worked for me and accommodated Lulu's dad's holiday plans, but we could also have all our

Christmas shopping taken care of by the end of November. By shopping at the Outlet Mall on our way home from my sister's, we would be ready to hang the tumbleweed and do our gifts exchange right on time. Things were really taking shape. Lulu agreed and Sally barked her consent.

From behind the wheel, I announced my intention to transfer the tumbleweed from lot to car. Looking back, perhaps I underestimated the task. Lulu seemed unimpressed, but succumbed to my urgings when I threw the car into Park, yanked out the key, and leapt out hooting "First one to catch it gets a gift certificate at Big Dog." Big Dog himself beckoned from a strategically-placed billboard looming on the skyline above the mall.

"Mom, it's rolling over to that field!" Lulu shouted, reminding me that tumbleweeds have a life of their own on a windy November day. I was bleary-eyed from driving. As I paused to see where she was pointing, she punctuated her sentence with "Made ya look!" and took off running, visions of Big Dog apparently dancing in her head.

It took me a minute to react. She was, after all, athletic at anything she tried, and clever to boot, having learned a thing or two about negotiating from her businessman dad and her attorney stepmom. Feeling competitive, I leapt into action, accidentally leaving the car door open, a situation of which Sally took full advantage. She leapt from the car and romped with us, golden fur flying in what was turning out to be a mildly hurricane-esque kind of day. The wind was so strong that the tumbleweed was rolling uphill, with Lulu, Sally and me right behind it.

The sound of the siren arrived as a blur in the wind. That was followed by a voice over a loud speaker. "Ladies, this is not an off-leash area. Come down from the hill. Return to your vehicle immediately." A police officer stood in the parking lot, bullhorn pressed to his mouth. Lulu, looking horrified, stopped in her tracks. As for me, a Berkeley girl at heart who had faced her share of police during demonstrations and, years later, having professionally conferred with them regarding subduing psychotic patients at the psychiatric hospital where I worked, I was in my element. I stood my ground.

"I don't believe it is posted, officer," I shouted in his direction. "We'll be down in a minute, after we catch this tumbleweed."

"Mom," Lulu chastised. "He's the police, let's go." Over the years, I'd taught my daughter to respect the law, primarily by slowing down whenever I sighted the black-and-white on the freeway, and by being polite in those unusual instances when the police car was unmarked and I got caught. I taught by doing.

"Sweetie, we are not breaking the law," I assured her. "Let me handle this." I was determined to get that tumbleweed. The police officer walked toward us, and I wondered if I had gone too far. Lulu stood beside me, clutching Sally by her collar. I smiled generously, noting the man's name tag flashing in the sun. I took my hands out of my pocket, displaying the absence of weapons. I knew the drill.

"Ma'am, it's Arizona law, and it doesn't have to be posted. All dogs must be on leash in commercial areas. Now send your daughter and your dog back to the car and let me help you catch this darn tumbleweed."

Lulu headed down the hill with Sally, and the officer and I worked as a team to surround the tumbleweed and grab it. He directed me to wait at the bottom of the hill, while he stood behind the tumbleweed and coaxed it down to where I stood. I swept it up into my arms and we walked back to the car laughing. I couldn't help but notice the Arizona tan on those strong arms, his broad shoulders accentuated by his uniform. His eyes reminded me of steel, and his graying hair seemed just right. Sadly, he wore a gleaming gold band on his left hand.

We scrunched the tumbleweed into the car, taking care not to break its branches, and Sally was forced to join Lulu in the rear seat. I offered the policeman the phantom gift certificate at Big Dog, which he passed on to Lulu. At this point, she was beaming her best golden-girl smile. "I've always taught my daughter to respect the law," I insisted, although I remembered fondly those days when I had stood among hundreds of anti-war demonstrators yelling "Off the Pigs!"

I thanked him for his help in corralling our Christmas tree and his eyebrows furrowed in apparent confusion. He shot a glance at my car, as if unable to ascertain my meaning, yet too wise to ask. He took a deep breath and looked at me, eyebrows raised, as if to ask, "Okay, what's next?"

I smiled reassuringly. "Thanks for keeping the peace."

We shook hands, and he walked away shaking his head.

Shortly thereafter, we arrived at my sister's, sat down to a beautiful Thanksgiving meal, and gave thanks for the love of family and the surprises along the way. We hung out in our pajamas, played Apples to Apples, and visited Big Lots on Black Friday.

Two days later, we returned to the scene of the crime, executed our Christmas shopping seamlessly in the mall, Lulu spending over an hour in Big Dog, and with all the packages stacked on the passenger side and Lulu and Sally seated behind the tumbleweed, drove back to Berkeley. Even in bumper-to-bumper traffic, I felt the joy of the moment, singing "Let it Be" along with the Beatles.

DEFENSELESS

I felt Maylie's presence when I heard the whoosh of her robes brushing against the stairs that led to the zendo, the formal structure at the Zen Center.

I sat inside, meditating with twenty others, missing the woman who had been my teacher for five years. She had died the day before, in Arcada, where she had gone to become the founding Abbess of a Zen temple. In the zendo, hearing that sound, I sensed that her spirit had come to check on us, as if she were outside the redwood door waiting to say goodbye. I felt connected to her as we exited the zendo and bowed out. I noticed a crow on the fence, black feathers glistening in the early morning light. I walked in its direction and it began to caw like a baby demanding to be fed. My throat tightened as a flash of pain arose from my stomach. I took a deep breath and felt the pain release as I exhaled and walked by.

Maylie had died quickly from a sudden illness. A Buddhist priest, she had taught about life's nearness to death. When it came, she seemed willing to go. The end came too soon for those of us who loved her. She had taught me zazen, sitting meditation, and I had learned to follow my breath, which centered my body and mind in the present moment. Sitting on my cushion, I came to trust the daily reprieve I found there. For those forty minutes I felt peace of mind, which helped when I had to work my way through a complicated divorce and raise my daughter as a single parent.

I had found my apartment after my divorce by writing an ad for my ideal living situation, an assignment in a computer class. I wanted to be in a house with a fenced yard, magnificent trees, and light streaming through large windows onto hardwood floors. I hardly noticed that I had received what I asked for. This apartment was surrounded by squirrel-enlivened pine trees and had a spacious deck. It was the upstairs rear apartment in a large red Victorian house. And next door to the Zen Center. What could have been better?

My six-year-old daughter Lulu and I arrived with few possessions, very little money, and a blind hope that things would get better. My hopeful disposition was a survival skill that was deeply ingrained. Maylie said my arrival at my new home was the result of Grace, which I had come to understand as divine energy creating possibilities and assistance when none were visible. I was comforted by this belief.

Throughout Lulu's childhood, I slipped out every morning at five-thirty while she slept and walked in the fresh morning air, through the adjoining garden, to the zendo, where for forty minutes I sat, breathing into my belly and letting go, again and again, of the doubt that sometimes consumed me. After meditation came chanting, bowing, and walking meditation, and through this daily ritual I was able to release the urgency and pressure that all too often seemed to characterize my life. In the bowing, as I touched my head to the floor, I gave myself over to a deep gratitude.

During the time I was Maylie's student, my parents, in their eighties, had died three years apart. Both died quickly and easily, and I found solace in prayers from my childhood. I continued my daily meditation and marveled at what others called my equanimity, an apparently valued Buddhist state, manifesting as emotional composure. Despite how others saw me, I was confused. Did meditation transcend grief? Or did it mask it? I was grateful to be saved from experiencing this painful feeling. Maylie helped me to see that the deep quiet of meditation was much like prayer, and I thought about my solitary walks in the forest as a child in Indiana. I felt safe and protected among those trees, as I now did in the zendo.

I remembered these things as I drove north to attend Maylie's passing ceremony in Arcata. When I arrived, I pulled into the driveway of an ordinary house and a small zendo, the crunching of gravel announcing my arrival. I saw several friends from the Zen Center who asked me to join them in a walking meditation along Maylie's favorite path in the nearby forest. As I walked, I felt the quiet of the redwoods, like wise elders standing by, witnessing our movement through their midst. I wondered if Maylie was near as I walked where she walked. Knowing I must say goodbye to her today, I thought of the crow's caw and felt, again, the flash of pain.

We returned from the walk and entered the recently built zendo, sunlight entering through high windows and causing the wood floors to shine. Around the perimeter were the familiar black zafu cushions, their round forms placed on the square and flat zabutons pads. Some fifteen people were sitting cross-legged on them and facing the wall. In the center of the room lay Maylie, so peaceful in death.

I joined them and was comforted by the silence and the community, as I immersed myself in memories of our friend. Soon I felt the loosening of my thoughts, and I focused on my breathing as well as the mantra Maylie had taught me: *"In, out/ deep, slow/ calm, ease/ mind, release/ present moment, wonderful moment."* After forty minutes, feeling calm and centered, I arose and walked to the middle of the room, where she lay on a raised wooden slab, dressed in her priest robes, elbows bent to allow her hands to meet over her belly in the traditional *mudra*. I stepped in line with the others who were in a walking meditation around her body. I stared at her face, so familiar, remembering the kindness that always emanated from her eyes, and the fearless transparency she embodied. I was glad to be with her. It felt right to be one of the many surrounding her with love. I felt only gratitude. I wondered if this was what was meant by equanimity.

Later that day, we were called from the zendo and asked to surround her pine box in a final gesture. She was to be transported in a truck-bed to the flames that would transform her to ashes, releasing her soul. People spoke and chanted and bowed. I was unable to speak or say goodbye, but felt peaceful, knowing I carried her memory with me.

I returned to my car and began driving down the coast toward Berkeley. Suddenly, the pain in my stomach returned, rose to my chest, and I cried out, overcome with sadness. Sobs pushed their way up my throat. I pulled over, stopped beneath a gathering of redwoods and sat in my car, leaning over the steering wheel. The outpouring overtook me and I lost track of time, submerged in this ocean of feeling. Exhausted, I leaned into my bucket seat and slept until I was awakened by a massive exit of crows, their loud shrieks and battering wings blocking all sound, the sky momentarily darkened by their presence. And then they moved on.

Continuing my drive home, I was hit with a feeling of joyous recognition; as if I had just rediscovered a part of myself I had forgotten. In claiming my lost despair, I was filled with compassion for the child and young person I once was.

Soon I discovered the Oakland Center for Spiritual Living, a church which integrated my feelings with my meditation practice. There I felt at home with the Gospel music which filled me with joy and sadness, as I rose to my feet, clapping and singing, at one with my body and my voice. The quiet of meditation took me deeper into myself and the music allowed me to express in song what had been denied and unspoken. As my feelings came alive in my daily life, I felt connected to the indwelling spirit. Perhaps that is what is meant by equanimity.

THE GREEN DRAGON

What I was about to do had once been out of character for me, but years of living in Berkeley had changed me. I knew there were those who wouldn't understand my choice, but several women at the hospital where I worked had my back, saying "Go ahead, try it!" and so I thought I might just take the leap. Four years into the twenty-first century, and I was fifty-nine, happily single, and in need of some excitement. Though sixty is just a number, I didn't like the sound of it. Perhaps a tattoo would keep me young.

It was Lulu's idea. She was fifteen and had been begging me for months. "Please, Mom," was her plea. "Crystal's mom did it, they both did, so let's do it together. It could be one of those mother/daughter bonding things." Crystal's mom was a single parent like me, though at fifty she was apparently dealing pot as her day job, and partying all night, so I didn't find Lulu's argument all that persuasive. I also knew that once we went down this path, there was no turning back. The effect was permanent.

Nevertheless, I love my daughter and have never ignored a bonding opportunity, so I read the business card Lulu handed me. It said *Green Dragon Tattoo: Body art, piercings and cover-ups.* My mind shifted at once to thoughts of criminal activity, and I felt a touch of terror, until I realized that cover-ups only meant they could make their work disappear. Maybe that was supposed to be reassuring.

Lulu had done her research. Tattooing is legal in Nevada for anyone age sixteen and over, while California's legal age is eighteen. It was clear from her constant urging that a tattoo was what she wanted for her sixteenth birthday. A trip to Las Vegas and the Green Dragon Tattoo Parlor would fulfill her dream. Given that half of Berkeley High freshmen arrived with numerous tattoos and piercings, this was a modest request on Lulu's part. Though I didn't feel driven to start a movement to lower the legal age to sixteen, I preferred that she have it done by professionals. Since I was leaning toward agreeing, I wondered if I could make it more palatable by getting one for myself. My sixtieth birthday was a week after Lulu's sixteenth, and I wanted to celebrate big time. Perhaps a discreet work of body art would be the perfect entrée into this new decade. It seemed like a great way to honor our mutual birthdays.

As I considered the decision, my voice of reason persisted. Getting a tattoo seemed dangerous. I would be the first in my family to have one, the first among my friends. Certainly no one at the Zen Center had a tattoo, at least not that was visible to me as we sat together meditating every morning.

Had I been unduly influenced by Lakeshia, a nurse at work who had a stunning shoulder tattoo from the Ashanti tribe? She encouraged the tattoo idea and told me that expressing herself with a tattoo at sixteen had kept her from doing drugs and having wild careless sex. Would it have a similar effect on Lulu? I'd been raised to believe that a tattoo was the *precursor* to drugs and promiscuity. But then, I'd also been raised to believe that smoking a joint led immediately to heroin addiction, and that hadn't happened. Weighing the risks for myself, I figured I was probably safe. As for my daughter, I found it unlikely that body art would thwart her development or lead her down untoward paths. She's a smart kid.

When I thought about the tattoo, I was sure I didn't want matching rose curly-cue designs, like Crystal and her mom had chosen. This tattoo was meant to help Lulu express herself, not claim allegiance to me. So, after due diligence, I made my commitment and began to plan our trip to Las Vegas.

Lulu joined in the process and went online to check out the Green Dragon Tattoo Parlor. "These people really rock," she declared. "It says that if we ask for Talons, Bikerboy, or Josh, we'll get great service."

I thought I'd go with Josh.

We pulled into the Motel Six on Tropicana Avenue, right across from the MGM Grand and Hooters, checked in, and went to our room. The double beds took up most of the space, but it was clean. Exhausted from the drive, I went right to sleep. When I awoke the next morning, Lulu was already up, having gotten free coffee and donuts from the front desk. I took hard-boiled eggs, a grapefruit, and V-8 juice from my cooler and insisted she have milk with her donut.

We found the Green Dragon Tattoo Parlor hidden away in an alley. On the upside, however, alleyways in Las Vegas are more strip mall corridors, and not dark and dirty pathways between apartment buildings, with fire escapes for quick getaways. I did, however, wonder what was in the dumpster next to the door emblazoned with a green dragon staring at us with red eyes. And was that a foot in the boot I saw peeking out of a black plastic bag? Lulu ignored all of my concerns and scooted inside to study the rows of tattoo designs lining the walls. I followed her in and scanned the room, which had white walls and a black linoleum floor. It seemed clean, even cheerful. A tall good-looking man with a ponytail and tattoos covering muscular arms grinned at me. "I'm Josh, may I help you?"

"Yes, please," I stammered, despite my relief that he was not Talons. "We'd like a tattoo." I felt Lulu cringe.

Lulu slid between Josh and me and began a very impressive discussion of Tribal versus Celtic versus Asian designs. For a minute, I thought they were talking about music, but since I didn't hear any, I just tried to look cool. I fixed my eyes on a spot on the wall, hoping to settle the nausea that was threatening to erupt. I felt like an adolescent stuck in a small space with the wrong crowd.

Josh directed Lulu to the Asian wall. I asked if they had any flowers, quickly adding that I didn't care for roses. I was escorted to a corner with a small display of hummingbirds, spider webs, black roses, and moons in various phases.

"Take your time and let me know if you have any questions," Josh said and then he walked away. I searched and found only one flower I liked, an iris. The problem was that it had a fuzzy stamen protruding from a dark opening, which looked uncomfortably phallic. I asked Josh if they made adjustments to their designs and he assured me that they could. He seemed amused, which made me feel even more awkward, as if I had asked permission to remove his penis.

"Does the process hurt?" I asked, thinking I was changing the subject.

"It feels like a repeating pin prick," he said, as if it were nothing.

"I have a low pain tolerance. Do you use anesthetics?"

To his credit, he kept a straight face. "We aren't licensed anesthesiologists, so no, we don't, but we can go slow. And of course we can stop any time you want." I imagined Josh getting only as far as the fuzzy stamen and black hole and then my backing out, forever marked by this experience. I saw Lulu roll her eyes and wondered if she'd read my mind.

Lulu ended up choosing a cala lily graced by a blue and yellow butterfly. She called me over to the desk so I could fill out the paperwork. I explained that she was sixteen, and she showed her ID. I scanned the liability contract and then I signed.

"If you take off your blouse," Josh said, as he directed me to the service area, "it will be easier to do the work. And it's important that you don't move." His voice was steady. I stripped to my tank top, sank face down into what seemed like a massage chair, and reminded myself that I was doing nothing wrong. Josh worked on me and Bikerboy, a short, stocky man with a shaved tattooed head, introduced himself and began working on Lulu. When I shot an anxious "Are you okay?" to Lulu, she snorted "Of course." Josh and Bikerboy were silent, absorbed in their art. Talons apparently had the day off.

I asked Josh to remove the stamen and close the black hole. His voice was convincing when he agreed. The sound of the electric needle steadily pulsating, injecting ink in quick spurts, reminded me of a sewing machine on its fastest speed. I can't say it hurt; it was more of a hard-core tingle.

Twenty minutes later, I leapt up from the chair, breathless. I felt daring and rebellious, and had to stop myself from shouting, "Here I am!" I couldn't wait to show Lakeshia. Lulu stood up and we compared our tattoos, silently grinning. Josh and Bikerboy smiled and I felt a thrill when Josh winked at me. I briefly considered asking them to join us for lunch, but reason prevailed.

As we walked to the car, I felt dizzy with possibilities, imagining the new outfit I'd buy to reveal my left shoulder and its new tattoo. Or maybe the convertible I'd rent to drive around town with windblown hair, wearing a strapless dress. Was it possible that I was having a mid-life crisis? Or was sixty just the new sixteen?

Lulu was oblivious, lost in her fantasies, but, as usual, cool as her favorite lime slurpee.

WARRIORS IN TRANSITION

I support the theory that teenage brains aren't developed enough to make high-level decisions, like joining the Army. But when the recruiters, Marin and Blue, came to my door, I invited them in. They were young, handsome, and self-assured. As it turned out, they already knew my eighteen-year-old daughter, Lulu, and had come to bring me into the fold. Lulu sat quietly at the dining room table, leaving it up to them.

I was in shock, so I took it in, uncharacteristically immobilized. As a sixty-two-year-old woman, I had expected more wisdom from myself, but none was forthcoming. I remember how they had mentioned killing the enemy in the same breath as world travel and five-digit paychecks. Unable to rally with any kind of response, I suggested they come back and talk further with my friend, Jorge, a veteran who had spent three years in rehab after his discharge from the Army, but they didn't think it was necessary. Neither did Lulu. I felt alone, my shallow breath cocooning me, feeding a creeping sense of isolation. It was May, 2007. The numbers killed in Iraq mounted daily.

Blue was clearly invested. "She's Army material," he said, looking Lulu up and down. He had apparently been texting her to arrange "workout meetings" for the last month. Lulu was a natural athlete, skilled in every sport she tried, and always a team player. She had a strong spirit and often kept her feelings to herself. Shuttling between two homes since first grade—her father's and mine—she had adapted by making the most of her time, though she often joked that she felt like a ping-pong ball. Sometimes she'd admit she hated it and then she'd return to what she called "toughing it out." Aside from eye rolls, occasional grumbling, and a repertoire of teenage body language, she was even-tempered and flexible. Low maintenance, she described herself. Did that make her Army material?

I remembered how she had become a vegetarian at age eight, after seeing a hand reach into a fish tank at Hong Kong East Ocean Restaurant in Emeryville to retrieve someone's dinner. I also recalled how, at twelve, she vehemently let go of her dream to be a veterinarian after our golden retriever, Sally, was put to sleep, stating she would have no part in any animal's death. How had she come to embrace killing human beings? Was it when she spent her last two years at Berkeley High attending a training course put on by the Air Force Auxiliary in San Francisco? She said she wanted to learn to fly, and she did, but what else did she learn? Perhaps I was in denial. I just didn't see this coming. With all due respect to those who serve and sacrifice, I had issues with the military.

Lulu's response to my concerns was reasoned and firm. "Mom. I'm eighteen; I don't need your permission." It was a cold moment.

She did agree to my request to write out her reasons for wanting to join the Army. In a nutshell, they were about community, service and discipline. These were honorable goals for a girl leaving home.

Just as I left Indiana for Berkeley in the sixties to the call of the civil rights and anti-war movements, she was leaving at a time in history where terrorism was in the daily headlines and bullying commonplace. She wanted to do something meaningful and find her place. Berkeley High had not provided that, and she doubted that college could either.

She began the ten-week Basic Combat Training immediately after graduation in late June, requesting that I cancel her admission to Cal State Monterey. There were regular calls and letters from her at Fort Jackson, South Carolina, where she reported on daily routines, friends she'd made, sports she played, even the guns she'd shot. In her estimation, the Army was the perfect life.

She liked the Army's high priority on family, and said she had chosen me as her family hero in a ritual performed by her unit. I was flattered but confused. I didn't feel heroic. I tried to accept this gift unconditionally, blanketing myself against the grief and fear that were always with me.

After Boot Camp she went to Fort Rucker, Alabama, for her Advanced Individual Training (AIT) in Air Traffic Control, a twenty-four-week program where she met and fell in love with a fellow soldier, Max. Surprising me yet again, they decided to get married within three months. I met him at their wedding in Alabama in January of 2008 and saw why Lulu loved him. He was the artistic son of a military father who wanted him to play basketball. Max loved that Lulu beat the pants off him every time they shot hoops, and she loved that he could draw and paint effortlessly and cook with equal artistry. They seemed to fit together like two pieces of a jigsaw puzzle, each making the other clearer by their connection.

I felt reassured knowing Max was there, and I went on with my life, gradually able to step out of auto-pilot and regain a sense of connection to my friends.

I was caught off guard when I received a brief call from the Army three months later informing me that Lulu had been transferred from her Air Traffic Control training to a program called "Warriors in Transition" for injured soldiers at Fort Gordon in Augusta, Georgia. My throat closed in fear, and I couldn't find my breath. What had happened to my child? And what were her injuries? The darkness in my mind stopped any hopeful thought from surfacing.

I called and was put through to her.

"Mommy." Lulu's voice on the phone was as strong as ever. "I'm fine. It's all Army kids here, most of them my age, some for drugs, some for depression, like me."

Depression? I had no idea. "Sweetie, can you tell me what happened?"

There was a long silence and then she began cautiously. "Mom, I wish you were here. I'd rather tell you in person." I wanted to grab her and shake her and demand to know. Fortunately, there were two thousand miles between us. Lulu had always hated talking on the phone.

"If you want me to come, just say the word. I'll be there on the next plane."

"The word," she said. "I gotta go. They're serving lunch. Love you." And she hung up.

I flew out of San Francisco the next night on the red eye, arriving at ten in the morning at Ft. Gordon, Georgia. Amazingly, I slept soundly on the plane. I felt nothing when I awoke, except a compelling need to see my daughter. It reminded me of a time Lulu and I had hit an extreme fog bank in Monterey driving home from vacation. I could see only two feet in front of me. Nothing could have distracted me from the task at hand; there were lives at stake.

I felt dwarfed by the massive stone edifice with "United States Army" etched on the granite entrance. As the door clicked behind me, I felt my shoulders rise in dread. I was referred to the psych unit, where I signed in. Before going to see Lulu, I blurted to the charge nurse, "How is she? Is she suicidal?" I blushed, knowing it was privileged information. I worked in a hospital. "I'm sorry. I'm just so worried."

Charge nurses have seen it all. She touched her heart and smiled warmly, saying, "She's waiting to see you. She's so happy you could come."

I walked down the hallway, pushing away the images of patients I had worked with who had survived suicide attempts. I thought of those who had not, including my boyfriend, Gerry, when I was only two years older than Lulu.

Lulu jumped out into the corridor and laughed when I gasped in surprise. She looked relaxed, wearing blue jeans and a black hoody, her uniform in Berkeley before she changed to the required Army camos in boot camp. Her hair was short and light brown, no pink or purple faux-hawk. "Straight-edge punk; cool without drugs or alcohol," she used to explain to those who asked.

"Hi, sweetie." Was it possible that everything was okay? We hugged.

She showed me to the empty day room, where she plopped down on a green leather sofa. "Mom, massage my head, will you, please?" A familiar ritual when she was stressed, it seemed like a good start. I kneaded my fingers into her scalp, alternately pulling gently on her hair. "So, Mom, I need you to just listen, okay? Hear me out."

I knew how Lulu often paused to think while talking, unnerving for me given my think-out-loud style. At my worst, I interrupted the silence with questions and she shut down. "I will," I told her, straining to remain patient.

This time she found her pace quickly, pausing only to clench her teeth when her eyes glazed over. "They put me on suicide watch for no reason," she said. "After I told a nurse that I was depressed about Max going to Iraq. His class graduated three months before mine, and they still treated us like we were single, living in different barracks and all. I had to stay in my room twenty-four-seven, with my roommate guarding me. No phone, no visitors. I asked to see a counselor when I couldn't sleep." She shifted uncomfortably, then turned to face me with renewed courage. "When I told her I was depressed, she didn't say a word to me, just smoked her cigarette and looked at her watch. Finally, she asked if I wanted to kill myself, and when I said "No," she told me to go back to my room."

I was furious. An image flashed in my mind of a psychiatrist at my workplace who fell asleep when talking to patients. Nothing was ever done about it, despite staff write-ups. Had I thought the military would do better?

"Then I was called into a meeting with ten male sergeants," Lulu continued. "They said I had defied authority by getting married. I'd heard that ten other couples had applied for marriage licenses after we did. According to the sergeant, Max and I had broken the rules by not filling out the paperwork correctly." She began working her fingers into the muscles of her neck, her voice imploring. "That was a lie, because we did it by the letter."

I had seen the paperwork and Lulu was right, it had been approved. Had she been set up as an example for others? I was a witness at their wedding, conducted by Judge Gammill, Justice of the Peace for Coffee County, Alabama. I carried a picture in my wallet of Lulu, Max, and the judge standing in front of a mounted deer head, the horns appearing to sprout from Max's head. He got a lot of ribbing for that. "I know you were hoping to be deployed to the same site," I said. "Is this still going to happen?"

Lulu shook her head and looked miserable. "The sergeants said the Army wouldn't recognize our marriage. They said Max would go to Iraq and I would never see him again. When I got back to my room, I threw out all my food and water, and swore

I wouldn't eat, drink or speak again until I could see Max. My roommate told on me. I don't blame her," she quickly added, her eyes wide, as if startled by the memory.

As she spoke, I was blessing the roommate.

"That's when they sent me here," she explained, and then she became silent, as if deep in thought. After a time, she said, "Max is coming to visit tonight; he leaves for Iraq in a week." Her face crumbled, tears spilling from her eyes. "I wasn't strong, Mommy, I wasn't a warrior."

My heart ached. "You were trying to express your pain the best way you could," I told her. "That takes warrior courage."

As we sat together in silence, I found myself building a legal case in my mind. My daughter was being harassed: they isolated her, they took her phone, and they denied her a legal marriage. "Do you think you were suicidal, like they said?"

A wrinkle appeared on her brow. "I'd never kill myself, Mom. I just felt desperate when I couldn't get any help and couldn't reach anybody."

Relief ran down my back. I was struck by her new emotional vulnerability. Through this ordeal, she had grown stronger, more able to express her feelings. She seemed freer to be herself. And perhaps, I, hopefully, had become a better listener. *Only good can come from this,* came a voice from deep inside. "I know," I told her. "You were desperate to connect with help and were denied at every turn. That is a terrifying feeling."

Lulu looked at me and smiled. Though the future was unknowable, we sat together in a comfortable silence. As the afternoon light changed from bright to soft tones, I saw her relax and I began to feel surprisingly at peace.

When Max arrived, looking handsome in his uniform and standing six-four, I wanted to leave them to be together. Before I walked into the hall, I hugged him and whispered, "I'll hold you in my thoughts and prayers until you return safely to Lulu's arms."

I walked out of the building, remembering Lulu's decision to join the rugby team in her senior year of high school. She had seemed to relish the danger, thrilled to risk injury. Today she was a more secure, softer young woman. At that moment, a red-winged blackbird landed in my path, black feathers and scarlet shoulder patches reflecting the sunlight. After strutting and puffing its chest, it surged skyward to join the migration of its flock. I'd read that red-winged blackbirds band together, closing ranks to form a mass that cannot be penetrated by predators. This flock seemed to possess a fierce and instinctive loyalty as they journeyed through the sky.

Watching the one merge with the many, I knew that Lulu's unfolding was just as it was meant to be. I basked in the knowledge that divine protection comes in many forms and that all life is interconnected. I understood that despite my feelings of fear and isolation, I am never really alone.

Two months later, Lulu was honorably discharged from the U.S. Army as a married woman. Although no legal action was taken to make this happen, U.S. Congresswoman Barbara Lee had paved the way at Lulu's request. Max served one tour in Iraq and was honorably discharged a year later.

PART FOUR

2010-2014

WILD TURKEYS RISING

The gang of wild turkeys stopped me in my tracks. Numbering close to ten, they strutted on skinny legs across the landscaped parking area foraging for insects and other edibles, yellow beaks poking the ground with unswerving attention. With long, red spotted necks and robust bodies feathered in black and white, each bird spread a dramatic arc of brown tail feathers. They were a regal sight, stunning in the fading afternoon light. Though they now lived in the wooded hills behind the two-decade-old county hospital where I had worked for fifteen years, they displayed audacious ownership of the developed land, reclaiming what had once been solely their territory. I watched them in awe.

My thoughts turned to my impending retirement. In three months, I'd honor my sixty-sixth birthday with new freedom. I was working full time as a psychiatric social worker, a direction I had taken in my forties, finding no practical use for my degree in English, and no longer feeling inspired by work as a paralegal. Mental health care called to me, most likely for personal reasons. My boyfriend Gerry's suicide and the discovery that he was bipolar was, for me, at twenty-one, formative. It took two decades before I followed my heart.

As a hospital social worker, I found working with suicidal patients fulfilling. I learned that the crisis that led to their hospitalization often forced them to re-examine their lives. Many found a sense of hope and empowerment that shifted their view of themselves and their future, and my own growth was deepened by their process. Over the years I spent on this job, I learned first-hand what drove Gerry as he faced the psychotic demons of his illness, which was often misunderstood in the sixties, and more easily diagnosed and treated in the nineties. Passionate about working with the families of those who where psychotically depressed, I found my niche in facilitating family support groups.

Ten years into my job, I spontaneously rediscovered writing, which I had abandoned after Gerry died. It reappeared in my life as a new way of connecting with myself and others.

On this day, as I watched the wild turkeys, I was filled with gratitude for all I had learned in the past fifteen years, affirming my choice at age fifty to transition from private practice to county-based care. I now welcomed the thought of retirement, looking forward to entering full time the domain of creativity. I knew it was time to move on.

I bowed in respect to the turkeys, got in my Honda Odyssey and headed toward the local car wash, wanting to put into motion the fresh start I was anticipating. As I waited in line, I put Tchaikovsky's Trio in A Minor in the car's tape deck, reclined in my bucket seat, my car idling, and immersed myself in what was, to me, the music of divine expression. Minutes later I rolled through the storm of water and exited the tunnel feeling pristine.

I arrived home an hour later than usual to

discover six police cars, a crime scene van, and two motorcycle cops on the corner where I usually parked. Half the block was closed off with yellow tape, and a crowd had gathered. I parked and walked toward the corner, where a neighbor told me there had been a killing from a two-car shootout an hour earlier. Nothing like this had ever happened in my south Berkeley neighborhood.

I saw the news helicopter buzzing overhead, and heard a woman screaming "He's dead! Oh my God, he's dead!" She sobbed inconsolably as she tried to break through the police line and get to the draped body, which was spread out across the sidewalk. The scene took me back forty-five years, to the morning when I received the call that Gerry was dead. Now, as then, I felt everything slow down; the air seemed strangely misty. The elm trees framed the woman, now lying on the sidewalk moaning, the police trying to calm her with quiet words. I was filled with sadness for both the family of the victims of this tragedy and for Gerry, a brilliant mathematician who, those many years ago, was lost to my world and to so many who loved him.

Standing there, police all around, I recalled the February morning when I received the news that he had leapt to his death at the International House, and how the police had driven me to the station to make a report. I had been the last one to see him alive and I had little to tell them, except that he had left my house the night before feeling discouraged. In some yet unrevealed corner of my mind, however, I knew there was more. I hadn't allowed myself to think he might be suicidal, but I was hit with an inexplicable sadness when he walked out the door. Earlier, when he told me he thought his brain was rotting, I assumed he was speaking metaphorically. After all, who wouldn't be anxious with upcoming doctoral exams? For years after, grief and guilt lurked like snakes in the crevices of my tender young mind, hibernating before their exit to the light. It took decades of therapy and meditation practice before I could forgive myself for not preventing his death, and to express the wild wail of my loss, as the woman on the sidewalk was now doing.

    I watched her tragedy unfold and realized that the shots had been fired in front of my parking space, and at the very time I regularly came home. Had I not deviated from my normal routine, I could have been in the line of fire. I was shaken by this truth. I was grateful to have been spared, having much to look forward to in my life.

    I felt Gerry with me, as if my unshakeable connection to him in life continued after his death. I understood that claiming and trusting the disowned feral territories in my psyche renews and deepens my connection with myself and others, allowing me to move forward and to integrate the past.

    The wild turkey suddenly appears in my mind, and I watch as it lifts itself skyward to return to its new home in the hills.

PICK AND PULL

I now keep men at a distance. As the youngest of three children in a conservative patriarchal family, I was schooled in catering to men's needs. Was it the internalization of feminist values that changed me? Or my nasty divorce? Or was it the fifteen years employed as a social worker sidekick to too many ego-driven male doctors? I don't know the origin of my withdrawal, but now most of my friends, my doctor, lawyer, therapist, spiritual teacher, chiropractor and dentist are women.

I prefer frequenting women professionals, and hanging out with women friends. As a babyboomer, I find women to be better listeners, reciprocal problem solvers, and often kinder and more empathic. At sixty-six, I find that interacting with men, let alone finding my second soul-mate, has fallen to the bottom of my to-do list. I have discovered the joy of meeting my own needs and making my own decisions without being entangled in the concerns of others. I can't imagine it any other way.

When I returned with my latte refill to my table in the garden room of the new café in Berkeley's Elmwood district, I hardly noticed the man who sat next to me. I had shifted my table into a windowed corner, creating an alcove overlooking the outdoor patio offering a lovely view of two ginkgo trees beginning to shed their lemon colored leaves. This created a childhood memory of a hideout which only I knew about. The thick golden Forsythia bushes which had edged our house had a secret entrance to the cave-like interior, creating a canopy. I had sat there, cross-legged, free to dream and imagine whatever I wanted, with no big brother or sister around with whom to compare myself.

At first I worried that this man's proximity threatened to interfere with my sense of solitude. I glanced at my new neighbor. He was writing in a notebook, and his table was similarly realigned to overlook the patio. He seemed to have a reserved self-containment, like mine, and I quickly forgot that he was there.

I opened my MacBook and began to revise an essay I was writing. At some point, there was a glitch with my laptop. After a couple of failed attempts to fix it, I considered interrupting him and asking for help. I noticed he was dressed in black athletic pants and shirt, black running shoes, a version of my own black walking outfit, and looked to be about my age, or perhaps a little younger. *A possible comrade?* I was amused at my wondering. "Excuse me," I finally said, "do you have a minute to help me?" I often ask directions or help from friendly strangers. I take pride in being self-sufficient, but I'm not too proud to ask.

He sported a graying buzz cut and a pale, slightly scarred complexion. "Sure," he said, making eye contact in a way that was attentive without being intrusive.

"I can't close this window." I moved my curser around and he observed.

He tapped a few keys. "I think if you just reboot it, it will be fine." I did as he suggested and it solved the problem. "It's the solution ninety-nine percent of the time," he added.

"It's like discovering that you forgot to plug in your typewriter back in the day,'" I said, hoping he wasn't so young he'd never used a typewriter.

He laughed quietly, his brown eyes framed with crinkly laugh lines, his smile modest. We went back to our work, sitting three feet apart, the window in front of us, yellow foliage and occasional floating leaves our landscape. I felt a kind of intimacy, like reading in front of a fire with a good friend; close by but in separate worlds. Almost like letting a fellow dreamer into my forsythia hideaway without a thought of being judged.

I was suddenly cold and put on my coat, looking around for the cause, unable to find it. A few minutes later, I looked up and saw that the man was closing a sliding glass door to the patio. I didn't bother to thank him, it all happened so quickly, and by the time I processed it he was already back to his writing.

Sometime later, I muttered, "Oh, no," worried about where I had parked. I turned and asked, "Do you know if this is a street sweeping day on Russell? I don't want to get a ticket." It seemed natural to ask him.

"I don't know, I didn't drive," he responded, which is when I realized that his clothes had the fit of bicycle attire.

"Oh, you're a cyclist," I said.

"Yes, that's mostly how I get around." He again smiled.

"That's wonderful. I hate cars."

"My car was just stolen," he said, and he proceeded to tell a story of how his car, an eighty-eight Toyota Camry, was the most frequently stolen car because many keys fit the ignition. He talked in an offhand way, but with a steady smile, his eyes lively as if he enjoyed the story. He related how the police recovered the stolen car, but it had missing parts. He went to Pick and Pull, a huge outdoor car parts mart in East Oakland. "You pay a ten dollar entrance fee and they will pick a matching model and pull the needed part off," he explained. "They sell it to you for next to nothing, and then two burly guys offer to install the part for an additional fee."

We laughed. "An offer you couldn't refuse," I said, and we laughed again.

I then told him about a friend who had insisted, against my objections, to replace the broken taillight cover on my ninety-seven Honda Odyssey, then left me waiting for months and never followed through. I was told about Pick and Pull by a young man in a black hoody. We were outside Grand Auto, shortly after I stormed out when I was quoted one hundred and twenty dollars for a taillight cover. "I never could get up my nerve to go to Pick and Pull, so I still drive with half a taillight."

He nodded. "I know what you mean; I took my brother along for protection."

We chuckled and returned to our work, but I found myself wondering what else we had in common. We sat quietly working for over an hour.

When I got up to leave, having decided I wouldn't interrupt him by saying goodbye, I was surprised when he caught my eye. "Do you come here every day? Is this your office?" he asked.

"No," I said, wondering why I had thought saying goodbye would be an interruption. "I usually work at home, but my Internet is on the blink. How about you?" I had forgotten that a conversation with a man could be engaging. And fun.

"I come here a lot. What kind of work do you do?" I told him I was retired from social work and had been writing for a few years, was working on a book. I noticed he didn't have a wedding ring. Maybe he was gay. He had a gentle quality. Were straight men more gentle these days? Had things changed without my knowing?

"I'm an artist," he said. "My wife is an editor. Maybe she can edit your book."

I admit I was disappointed to hear he was married, but took the reins on that uncomfortable feeling and switched to suspicion. Was he simply drumming up business for his wife? Was his kindness genuine? Or was I jaded? I hardly thought of myself as jaded.

"Only if she's kind," I said, and he nodded. I pulled out my card that said simply "Writer" next to my name and email address. I felt strangely giddy, as if I had willingly given away a part of myself. Was it a sign? Was I changing?

He handed me his card. "The address is wrong, but the email is current."

I looked at his card. The address was in London. "Wow, you've come a long way." He didn't have a British accent.

"I'm making a transition," he said. His body language was open, but his words were not.

"Ah," I said. "That can be challenging." A divorce? A job change? I didn't ask. Had I intuited that he preferred not to reveal much? Or was I afraid to ask, as if by asking I would reveal too much of me? I sometimes wonder if I know how to talk to men, having experienced the strong, silent types of my youth, the loud, argumentative ones in my family, and, unfortunately, the passive-aggressive one I had married. Men seemed to speak another language, giving them a foreignness that left me mute, or hyper-verbal with anxiety. Could I find comfort in just being myself with a man?

"Yes," he said, again revealing little and confirming my intuition.

"Well, I've got to get to my car before the meter maid does," I said, terminating the conversation.

"Yes, those tickets can be hefty." He smiled, the crinkles around his eyes reappearing.

Walking out of the café and into a burst of midday light, I felt the sun's warmth on my face, and I was hopeful. Had men changed? Or had I?

When connection with a kind-hearted man comes unbidden, I am reminded that they, too, are alive and well. Unless he was just drumming up business for his wife.

I laughed to myself, wondering if I could ever change.

DAYZHAVOUS

She stood beside her dented truck, hands on her sizeable hips, smiling widely, and displaying a mouthful of rotten teeth. "I'm Chez, short for Charlize," she said. "I'm the manager here at Dayzhavou Trailer Park."

I extended my hand. "I'm Ellen, Lulu's mother. Nice to meet you, Chez."

"Hope you're ready for this Kansas weather," she said, pushing a strand of burgundy hair out of her eyes. Before I could answer, she added, "I hear you came all the way from California to help your daughter move in." When I confirmed this and told her how happy I was to be there, she said, "It's a beautiful day for the kids to get started in their new trailer."

The kids? Did I detect a maternal tone? I hoped this was not another lesson the universe was surprising me with, to loosen up my own mother issues. Lulu had a birthmother, a mother (me), a stepmother, and a solitary aunt who was mother-identified.

Would I now be adding "trailer park mother" to the list? My head pounded with memories. I thought about my sister holding three-day-old Lulu for what seemed like hours when we visited her on our way back to California from Lulu's adoption in Kansas. My arms ached to hold my newborn, but I found myself mute in the face of an imagined show-down driven by a crazed possessiveness. Three weeks later, when the birthfather contested the adoption, I, again, had to fight my rage and allow my lawyer to take on what she did best.

Now, two decades later, Lulu and I were back in Kansas. She had married a Kansas boy and they were moving here to live near his family. I wasn't ignorant of the fact that Max's family lived an hour's drive from Lulu's birthmother, Carly, and the birthfather who had contested the adoption. I had not had contact with Carly in twenty years. Though Lulu had been contacted by Carly's son on her eighteenth birthday, she didn't pursue the relationship. I felt a creeping sense of dread, fearing that my connection with my daughter would be decimated. Would this ever end?

As she spoke, Chez glanced around her. Scattered over an area the size of a football field were perhaps fifteen mobile homes, all different sizes, colors, and states of repair. The stand-out was silver Airstream. It had two new motorcycles parked in its cemented yard, and a satellite dish attached to its roof. A nearby trailer was parked adjacent to a grassy lawn that boasted a garden with staked tomatoes and sunflowers. A few of the trailers appeared to be abandoned, their peeling paint and dust-blown yards strewn with cars, bicycles, and rusting lawn chairs. I felt uneasy as I viewed my daughter's new neighborhood. Chez's cell phone rang and she walked away. I was relieved to have this time to be alone, as I waited for Lulu to return with our lunch.

Lulu had found their mobile home on Craig's List. "Original owner, excellent condition, $2,000." She told me that it was the perfect solution after their landlord had imposed an outrageous rent increase, doubling what they had been paying. Lulu had orchestrated the move of the well-maintained, mobile home from Topeka to "Dayzhavou," a trailer park located at the end a dirt road off the main highway. The area was flanked by forest on one side and fields of golden grasses on the other, where a chestnut mare and her foal grazed. It reminded me of the pictures Lulu had drawn as a young girl growing up in Berkeley, dreaming of a rural life. I often wondered if Kansas was in her DNA.

Lulu arrived with our lunch and we made a place for ourselves under the shade of a tree. As we ate our sandwiches and sipped our diet cokes, we discussed what we needed to do next. At the top of the list was a trip to a store that sold the flaps that go around the bottom of mobile homes. Without them, the trailer looked unfinished, and to me, unloved. Chez reappeared, slapping her cell phone closed, and thrust herself into the conversation. "No need to buy those," she told us. "They're up in the barn. I'll open it for you." She ran her hand through a mop of shiny burgundy hair. "How do you like my hair? I just got it done." Her matching burgundy polyester pantsuit gleamed as well. "I'm an entreepenur," she said, giving the word an unusual pronunciation. "So I need to look the part, right?"

"Right," Lulu and I said simultaneously, followed by "Jinx, you owe me a diet Coke," and the three of us laughed.

We followed her up the hill to a dilapidated barn surrounded by waist-high grasses. As we stood there, she pulled a key ring from her large shoulder bag. There must have been twenty keys on that ring. One by one, she tried each key. "Goddamnit," she mumbled. "Which one of these fucking keys is it?"

Lulu and I exchanged eye rolls.

After more failed attempts, Chez threw the keys into her purse. "Go around to the back and let yourself in. The door should be open." With that, she turned and strode down the hill, hips and arms swaying, the purse slapping her side. When she reached the bottom, she hopped into her truck and drove off.

The back door had no lock on it. We pushed it open and Lulu called out, "Anybody here?" It was dark and I fully expected bats to fly out of the rafters and head straight toward my hair.

Silence. We were apparently alone.

Lulu walked inside. "Mom," she asked, "do you have a flashlight?"

I told her that I did not, and that I thought we should leave. "I'm scared," I admitted. "You don't know what kind of beings are in here: vermin, psychotic, whatever." I was unprepared for what might lay ahead, unnerved by chaotic feelings activated by the smallest of changes. My body sometimes felt like a pinball machine reacting with bells and lights.

"Mom, you're the one who taught me never to give up," said my daughter. "Chez said there was a light switch in the front." With that, she strode toward the front of the barn.

I froze in place, unable to move.

Lulu waded through piles of unknown objects. Suddenly the room filled with a dim light. "I think the flaps are over there," she said, pointing to a pile in the middle.

A closer look revealed hundreds of trailer flaps, some nailed together in strips, others single, all haphazardly strewn. We picked and chose, until an hour later we were covered with dust and in possession of a large pile of flaps. I began counting them, not wanting to haul out more than we needed.

"Mom, let's go," Lulu whined as she reached for a cigarette. In my mind I saw the whole barn go up in flames.

"Would you mind waiting until we're out of the fire zone?"

Lulu was abrupt, craving tobacco. "Sure, Mom, sure."

"So how can we move these things?" I asked.

"I wish we had Chez's truck." Lulu said.

I had studied the truck earlier. Hanging over the open tailgate were several graying eight-foot-long two-by-fours; inside the bed of the truck was a rusty water heater, collapsing cardboard boxes filled with paint cans and calking guns, as well as dried leaves and wadded MacDonald's bags and drink cups with straws intact.

"Do you think there would be room?" I wondered aloud, zipping my lip on what an out-of-control mess it was.

"Sure, there's room. Look, here she comes," Lulu shrieked as Chez sped up the hill to the barn, tossing out her cigarette nonchalantly. She hung out the window of her truck and shouted, "I'm back!"

Lulu waved and I scanned the weeds to see if the cigarette was sizzling in the dry grass, imagining the wind fanning the embers and my driving the hell out of there with flames at my tail.

"So, you ladies find the skirting?" Chez continued.

That's what it's called, I thought. Like the skirt that comes with the bedspread to cover up the dark underneath, or, in this case, where cinder blocks held the trailer off the ground. I guessed Lulu would be dry if there was a flood, but what about tornadoes? The darkness of my mood descended.

"Yes!" Lulu shouted back. "We've got a whole pile of them."

"Let's put 'em in the truck and I'll take 'em to your trailer," Chez responded.

I suddenly felt exhausted. I had forty-four years on Lulu. Chez looked to be in her forties; I wondered if she was on speed.

Chez jumped out, hoisted herself up onto the bed of the truck, and began pushing things around. I couldn't really see any progress. It was like pushing the liver and kale around on my plate when I was a kid.

"Come on girls, throw those suckers up here," she ordered. She flipped her hair and tucked it behind her ear with burgundy fingernails.

"Sure, Chez, we got it," I replied, as I tossed the skirting into the truck, my diet Coke kicking in. The single skirting pieces disappeared into the crevices, the larger widths rested precariously on top. I found myself wondering whether Lulu's intention to make a home for herself without her California family would fall between the cracks of Dayzhavous, or if her creativity and desire to do things on her own terms would carry her forward. I imagined her at family barbeques with Max's family. Maybe she'd even invite her birthmother, who would become friends with her mother-in-law, and they'd take Lulu on shopping trips together. I felt a clench in my stomach, the calling of old losses.

"Take a rest, Mom. You've got a long flight ahead of you tomorrow. Chez and I will finish this," came Lulu's authoritative voice.

I heard the wind rustle through the grasses while the chestnut horse whinnied to its foal. The bright sky was untouched by clouds. Where was that serenity in me? My daughter didn't seem to need me anymore and would never come home again. Where did I fit in? I felt alone and unwanted. The pain of past separations filled my heart.

I had promised myself at Lulu's birth that I would always love her exactly as she was, and never ask her to conform to my needs or expectations. The veracity of that commitment was being tested. Circumstances were stretching me beyond my familiar boundaries.

The full-length lawn chair under the weeping willow tree beckons to me and I approach it and sink in, stretching out to fully relax. I begin to breathe, slowly and purposefully, until I find the place of calm within, a familiar touchstone to the sacred where I feel connected and alive. Only then does a sense of pride well up in my heart as I watch Lulu create her nest, knowing she will feather it with her own experiences, as well as with the family memories we have built together. What more could I possibly want? The fear of losing my connection with my daughter disappears.

The next evening I settle into my bed, safely back in California. My phone rings. It is Lulu.

"Can you talk, Mom? I want to tell you something."

Oh no. What happened? "Of course. What is it?" How quickly I abandon my piece of mind. I breathe.

"Max and I met Carly today."

"Wow that was quick." Dizziness overcomes me and I feel nauseous. "How was it?"

"It was strange, Mom. She smelled like alcohol. She just kept talking about how sad she was that she gave me up. She said she and Richey, my birthfather, get drunk and have a huge fight every year on my birthday and someone always calls the police."

I wonder how Lulu must feel being told she is the cause of such fighting. I blurt out, "She must have wanted you to know how much she loved you," unable to tolerate my fury at not being able to control Carly's words, and wanting to make it better.

"It's her drinking, Mom," Lulu says matter-of-factly. "That's the alcohol talking." Lulu was no fool when it came to witnessing alcohol abuse. I had tried to teach her to take care of herself and to remember that alcohol distorts a person's reality. I wanted her to know how to protect herself from other people's drama.

"Mom, are you still there?"

"I'm here."

"Well, mostly I wanted to tell you that I am so glad you are my mom. I don't even want to imagine the crazy life I would have had if Carly had kept me. The good news is that I have a brother and he's in recovery and a really nice guy. He rarely sees Carly. He's married and has a son, and I can't wait for you to meet them the next time you come to visit. That will be Thanksgiving, right? It's only three months away. You can sleep on our sofa and look out the window at the horses."

"Sounds perfect." I say.

"Night, Mom." Lulu says, and we hang up.

I suddenly feel as if I have completed a marathon. I am relieved, exhausted, but wildly uplifted. Nothing had been lost. Not only has there been no rupture to my relationship with my daughter, we have grown closer. I feel myself opening to all the changes that lay ahead of me. Once again, I give in to the truth that I am not alone, but surrounded by a wise and loving universe. I am always protected, even when I have completely lost track of this fact. My breath deepens.

WE ARE FAMILY

Glorinda stood back as she flung open the narrow double-door of her four-by-six-foot walk-in closet and exposed what lay within. She turned with a smirk to catch my response. There were clothes piled almost six inches high on the floor. Leather, fabric and "pleather" purses and backpacks hung on hooks interspersed with multi-colored scarves and hats. A rod ran along the left wall and it was densely packed with blouses, suits, and full-length coats on plastic hangers. Above were ceiling-high rows of cubbies for shoes, many holding mismatched or solitary footwear: old-style Birkenstocks, knee-length black boots, worn white running shoes, and loafers in brown and navy.

I smiled. I knew this would take time, but we had it. We were both retired, and in our sixties.

Glo started to laugh. Furrowing her forehead edged with a graying afro, a raspy cawing sound emerged from her throat. She held her hand over her mouth in an effort to stop what had become a shriek as she bent over in a state of collapse.

I clutched my stomach, caught up in her laughter. "We can do this, Glo," I sputtered.

"I knew you'd say that, El, but will you please tell me how? I've been trying since New Year's Eve 2010 and here it is May Day 2011." Suddenly serious she stared at me wide-eyed, as if shocked by her confession.

"Easy. We just put everything from the floor onto the bed by category, and see what we've got. Then I'll go through the shoes, hats and scarves for duplications, out-of-style, and worse for wear, and you can look through your old work clothes and donate about half of them to Working Women Boutique."

"Have you got a couple of days?" she barked.

"We'll have this done in four hours tops. Trust me, I've done this before." Though I never made a formal business of it, friends knew I could handle household chaos, and I was called in from time to time. Demonstrating my commitment, I got down on my hands and knees, crawled into the closet and began tossing clothes to her.

"I bet you didn't know what you were in for, did you, El?" Glo caught the clothes I tossed and put them on the king-sized bed that she shared with her partner, Suzette, who was expected home by five o'clock. It was noon. "Suzette thinks I'm a lost cause."

"She's entitled to her opinion, Glo. But we all have our messy issues. This just doesn't happen to be one of mine, so it doesn't faze me."

"Look! I thought I had lost this." She held up a white Chico's shirt with a pleated gusset and stunning pearl buttons. It was still stiff with sizing but rumpled from lying on the floor. The price tag was attached with a tiny gold safety pin and a thin black cord. "This cost eighty dollars. I wonder if I can take it back?"

"Let's make a "possible return" pile here on the dresser," I suggested.

Glo stood in front of the mirror holding the shirt up to her chest, smiling and pivoting. Five-nine in her walking shoes, she was slim with small features and no visible make-up. She was amazingly unwrinkled at sixty-seven. "Don't you think it's pretty? I like a white blouse with black pants. It's such a crisp look."

"Yes it is. Why don't you put it on the dresser for now," I added firmly, imagining the endless fashion show Glo could put on. I continued to rummage through the closet, tossing clothes behind me like a dog flinging dirt.

My thoughts floated back to when Glo and I met in graduate school in the seventies. I was working as a legal secretary and she was working for San Francisco County Adoptions. We were both in the Counseling M.A program at San Francisco State. Our first clinical rotation was at SF General, where we were assigned a women's group to facilitate. Thrown into a group of six women who had arrived at the emergency room after having tried to harm themselves or others, I was so uncomfortable I almost walked out. Glo seemed right at home and had people talking in no time.

She took me aside after that first group session, and in a low voice that sounded almost conspiratorial, said, "I need to let you know I'm gay, in case you don't want to do a group with me," which was Glo's way of saying, "In case you are some kind of a homophobic nutcase, consider this fair warning."

I responded "So? Some of my best friends are lesbians." She flashed me her "no shit" grin and walked away.

I felt as if I were in the minority as a straight woman in the early days of the Bay Area women's movement, and wanted to be politically correct. Sleeping with men or being married was, in some circles, considered a sell-out. Political gatherings were for women only, and many were defining themselves as lesbian or bi-sexual. I rarely mentioned my boyfriend Charlie, happy to pass.

Glo was living the life of a closeted county adoption worker by day, while at night she created tall, elegant cylindrical sculptures, which she showed at galleries around the Bay Area. One of her shows had six of these goddesses gathered together, and when I stood near them they almost seemed alive. When Glo said they sometimes talked to her, I was intrigued. The art world was so different from the legal world in which I spent my days, and a creative spark of recognition arose in me when I was with her.

The pile on the bed was getting higher by the minute. I was beginning to doubt the wisdom of my plan. "Are you putting them in sections or something, Glo?" I couldn't see any delineation within the overall pile.

"I certainly am. Look a little closer," she hissed. I squinted my eyes and craned my neck and still saw one big blur. "Here are the dress pants, that's the dressy shirts. There are the casual shirts and pants. Here are the sweat pants. That's the sweatshirts." She extended her arm and pointed sharply. "And here, bless their hearts, are the t-shirts, long and short sleeve. Okay?" She drew out the "kay" with attitude, crossed her arms and waggled her head, daring me to disagree.

"Oooooh, I get it now. Good job!" I wasn't about to cross her.

She beamed. "Look at the closet floor! It's empty. I can't believe it. You'll be here every month, El. It won't stay this way. Besides, you still haven't done the shoes, scarves and bags. And I've got to part with half of those pantsuits." She barged into the closet, pushing me aside and pulled down armloads of suits. "These are ancient." She closed her eyes. "I just won't look. Just tell me where to put them for that boutique."

"Here." I opened a black garbage bag, and she dumped them in. She refused to part with any of her purses and backpacks, but hanging them all together next to the scarves opened up that wall. Together we attacked the footwear cubby, tossing shoes back and forth until most had found their mate, though there were still a few singles that we tucked together, hopeful that the other shoe would appear in time.

I wanted to make sure we got things put away before Suzette, a real estate agent, came home for dinner. I looked around, wondering where we would put the piles Glo had created.

"We can put that stuff in the armoire," Glo said, and she opened two huge mahogany doors to reveal six shelves that were only half-full. She squinted and said, "El, we are so different. I would never do this by myself. What's the glue to our friendship?"

"I don't know," I answered. "We've been friends for almost thirty years. You're my daughter's godmother. Loyalty?"

"I guess. We've certainly been there for each other through lots of losses," she said, looking down and shaking her head. "Your divorce, my breakup, those wonderful dogs and cats we've said goodbye to."

"Yeah, those were tough times. But you always inspired me. That crazy artistic mind of yours really spoke to me, until I began to believe I could make art with my writing. After a forty year dry spell." My throat filled with feeling. "It's that artistic chaos," I told her. "You tolerate it well and I don't." I learned that back when we did the women's group. I was terrified, but Glo just settled in, rubbed shoulders with those women's messes and drew out more of it. "Nothing seems to scare you, Glo, and I take refuge in that."

"And you are fearless about knowing yourself. You do all that meditation," she said, "and church, and therapy, and you just know who the heck you are, warts and all. Maybe that's why you don't judge me. You just take me at face value. I need that."

I dabbed at my eyes.

"Now don't you cry just because we need each other," she told me. "You depend on me because I'm not afraid of messes, and I depend on you because you know how to work with them. You just dive into what's in front of you, and I ignore it until it gets to be too much." Her eyes widened. "Sometimes I can't see my way out of it. I count on you for that. You embrace the chaos and find its inner order. It's that Zen thing you do."

My heart warmed at the recognition.

Glo, not one for quiet moments, interrupted my reverie, with a count-off. "One, two, three, four." She broke into Sister Sledge's "We Are Family." We locked eyes and nodded while Glo strutted around the bed pointing to the piles, which I picked up and jammed into the armoire, and she shimmied on down to pick up the pieces I had dropped, pushing them haphazardly on top of the others. Together we closed the door and turned the key.

After thirty years of friendship, the whole job took only three hours.

THE JOY OF COOKING

My mother wouldn't admit it if she were alive to tell, but I don't think she liked to cook. Especially dinner. She had her regular menus, which she prepared by herself and put on the table at six o'clock every night of the week. She said it was a woman's duty.

On Mondays, Mother served her family of five tuna casserole and a wedge of iceberg lettuce, dribbled with Thousand Island Dressing and flanked with tomato wedges. Tuesday it was pork chops, canned green beans, and a canned pear flaunting a maraschino cherry in the core, resting on an iceberg lettuce leaf. Wednesday's dinner consisted of liver and kale, as a testament to healthy eating, served with iceberg salad and Good Seasons Italian Dressing. Thursdays we had meatloaf, broccoli (from frozen), and banana salad--an iceberg lettuce leaf holding a banana sliced lengthwise, topped with peanut butter mayo dressing. Fridays it was fish sticks with tartar sauce and an iceberg wedge with Thousand Island. Saturdays there were hamburgers or Chef Boyardee Pizza that came in a box. On Sundays, Mother served baked chicken slathered in Kraft barbeque sauce, mashed potatoes, peas (from frozen), and the iceberg with Italian. Every week.

I don't remember these menus ever changing, except on birthdays and holidays, which explains my curiosity when I discovered a two-ring binder that I had shelved ten years earlier, without opening, part of a package of books Daddy had sent after Mother died. I hadn't been ready to feel the sadness I held about our relationship, which I feared her books might have brought up for me, but I remembered how I longed to connect with my mother as a young girl, and looked for ways we could share things. I helped her plant the marigolds in our window box, careful not to spill the dirt, and I threaded the bobbin at the sewing machine when she made my dresses. I also went grocery shopping with her, putting away and organizing the canned food when we came home. And even though she seemed distracted, I wanted so much to believe she was glad to have me around. But I often wondered, because although I set the table every night for dinner and sat with my family, I was painfully aware that I was unable to match my older brother and sister's tales of success at school: their straight-A report cards and their academic plans. Nor could I join in the father-son debates which often became arguments. Feeling excluded, I did what I did best: I watched the conversation bounce from person to person, creating pictures in my mind about the content of what they were arguing, and blending those observations with the feelings that ran through my body.

Sometimes I would lean over to share a thought with my mother, who always sat to my left. But she could furrow her brow or set her jaw as if biting back some feeling, and then turn to fill someone's ice tea glass. I felt flattened by being ignored by her, though later came to understand how upsetting and distracting it was for her when my father and brother argued. Daddy said I was a sensitive child with artistic abilities, but when Mother looked away I wondered if I wasn't smart enough or had too many feelings, or was just too quiet with too many pictures in my head. I didn't feel seen by her. It was as if we spoke different languages.

The binder appeared to be a cookbook assembled by my mother early in her married life. She had graduated college with honors in English, full of dreams of being a classroom teacher. Maybe it was originally one of her college binders. Or perhaps it was where she copied poems from her favorite poet, Elizabeth Barrett Browning, which she could recite by heart; or where she wrote the sonnets that she shared with me when I began to write free verse in high school.

Snapped into the two rings was lined paper, now yellowing with age and displaying recipes cut from the newspaper and scotch-taped neatly to the pages, along with carefully handwritten recipes. The tape had a dry translucent quality, as if insect wings had dried on the page, and there were mysterious oval brown stains at the bottom of some pages, like toeless footprints of a curious critter. Along the right side were one-quarter-inch tabs for each letter of the alphabet, and the opening page proclaimed, in my mother's distinctive backhand script, *Index* centered at the top. Below that, one line per letter, categories *A* through *R* listed types of recipes. *N* was blank. There was no apparent connection between the letter and the category, no obvious system. Or did she have one?

Under category *A* she had listed Raised Breads and Biscuits. Category *B* was for Baking Powder Biscuits and Quick Bread, boasting newspaper recipes for blueberry muffins, cornbread, banana bread, popovers, and doughnuts. For some reason, *C* designated Griddle Cakes, Waffles and Fritters. (I don't remember having anything for breakfast except cereal or scrambled eggs.) *D* was for Main Dishes, including Cube Steak Stroganoff, Chili Con Carne, New Orleans Ribs, and Hawaiian Chicken, none of which ever graced our table. *E* was Meat Sauces, all on one page, consisting of never-tasted Cocktail Sauce, Cheese Sauce, and Barbeque Sauce; and *F* boasted Vegetables beginning, oddly, with Baked Beans, followed by Rice, Potatoes, Onions, and Other Vegetables (including Green Beans with Almonds, Peas and Mushrooms. We did eat potatoes, green beans, and peas, though I don't remember almonds or mushrooms).

I felt baffled as I held the binder. What did it mean to her? Did she cook these things before I was born? Was the birth of her third child so overwhelming that she stopped trying new things, or did she only hope to make these dishes and never got around to it? I wondered if her chronic illness had affected her more than I knew. I continued to peruse the pages of never tasted recipes and finally recognized a dessert that my tongue and heart remembered: my mother's Gingerbread, which she served with Lemon Sauce. I found two full pages on Gingerbread. First was a clipping entitled "Gingerbread Donut Boy: When a

Glorified Donut Meets Up With Ice Cream," describing a treat we never made, a Gingerbread donut, ball of ice cream and gingerbread hat held in place by a candy stick. Flipping to page two, I teared up when it appeared: my beloved Gingerbread, written in her unforgettable script. I was carried back to a memory of helping Mother make that spicy cake, a spontaneous exception to her solo preparation, usually on a rainy day.

Beginning when I was eight, with me on the step stool at her side, I would assist in measuring the dry ingredients into the sifter, the flour mixing with aromatic cinnamon and cloves and pungent ginger. She would cream the sugar and butter, add the eggs, and put the bowl on the revolving mixer plate. Then I would slowly pour in the thick brown molasses and, when it was blended, I'd add the flour mixture. The grand finale was stirring in a cup of hot water. I was rewarded by licking the beaters from the electric mixer.

After Mother greased and floured the pans, I'd pour in the batter. She would give me a pot holder to push the pan into the oven, and when the timer dinged, to pull out the gingerbread and test it for doneness by pressing the top to see if it sprang back. There was not a lot of discussion, just doing and being. For those hours, I was all hers, and my brother and sister were nowhere to be found.

My face flushes with excitement as I located, under the letter *I* the Lemon Sauce that adorned the gingerbread cake. I could almost taste the tart sweetness of the faintly yellow sauce made from powdered sugar and fresh lemons, which mother pressed on the bulbous green juicer attached to the mixer. A perfect match for the gingerbread, it dribbled down the side of the cooled cake, and I sometimes ran my finger across the icing, pressing just enough to get a crumb of the gingerbread, and licked it off when she wasn't looking.

These memories were so satisfying that I didn't care that she never made the other dishes in the cookbook. Knowing that under *O* was my mother's Gingerbread recipe, and under *I* her Lemon Sauce, made the book a treasure that memorialized a time with my mother, a special moment when talking was not required and comfort reigned. A time when I believed she was happy to have me beside her.

Though we never made the Donut Boy, the recipe reminds me of a playfulness in my mother which I rarely saw. Perhaps she imagined lovingly preparing the Donut Boy with me, and then sitting down at the red Formica table to share this treat in a warm kitchen where the windows were steamy, enclosing us in our own world. Maybe our voices rang out with laughter as the Donut Boy's face melted and his hat fell off.

I will never know what drove my mother to make this collection of recipes, but I *do* know that she made an unforgettable gingerbread, and when she tasted her lemon sauce to top it off, she would purse her ruby Revloned lips, close her eyes, and smile with a kind of ecstasy that transcended duty.

Remembering that moment, I feel connected to her, knowing we created the gingerbread together. When asked to taste-test the lemon sauce, I can see myself putting a spoonful on my tongue, throwing back my head and crooning, speaking a language that only she and I understood.

BOOMERANG BABES

"Holy shit," my twenty-three-year-old daughter Lulu whispered loudly, closing the bathroom door behind her. Her husband Max had been in there for forty-five minutes and she was worried. They had moved into my home in Berkeley months earlier, in the summer of 2012, qualifying them as card-carrying members of the Boomerang Generation. Both of them had been honorably discharged early from the Army, but they said they had no regrets about their decision to join. After all, that's where they met.

"What happened?" I asked.

"He cut his hair and shaved."

"Wow!"

"And he took a shower. Isn't that great?"

"Nice," I responded, holding to my policy of not criticizing my daughter's husband, whose hygiene had visibly diminished since leaving the Army. Or was it just a response to Berkeley? A tall redhead with a chiseled face, he and green-eyed, blonde Lulu had made a stunning pair in their dress green uniforms and buzz cuts.

When Max had completed his army duty, they returned to his hometown in Kansas. After two years, they decided to move west. In many ways, Max was a Berkeley soul. A gifted draftsman and painter, he also loved to cook, was comfortable talking about his feelings, and was low-key and mellow. I liked his quiet nature, his well-honed intuition, and his free-spirit demeanor. In many ways, Max was a reminder of my youth as a

Midwest transplant to Berkeley. At sixty-seven, youth was something I increasingly valued.

And now, after traveling twice a year to various southern army bases, and enduring two years of back-and-forth trips to Kansas, I was amazed that Lulu was finally home, especially because I had given up hope that this would ever happen. I offered my "guest room" (Lulu's repurposed bedroom) until they could find jobs and save for their own place.

At first they misunderstood my proposal, which was "I'm no longer calling the shots; we're all adults and we'll all share the responsibility." My ban on cigarettes and pot on the property was accepted. They agreed to pay rent, maintain the common areas, have a household job, and spend time each day looking for outside work. I thought we were clear on all these points. I soon learned that the "we're all adults" part was questionable, and that being twenty-three may not be a guarantee of adulthood. In their view, they didn't have to keep me informed, they could borrow the car when they wanted it, and if they didn't like something, they could engage in mutual eye rolls.

I kept quiet in the beginning. They were, after all, getting unemployment checks and paying their share of the rent and food. Our schedules were different, so we ate separately. There were positive aspects to the overall set-up. For one thing, they maintained the common areas impeccably and had a way of disappearing just when I wanted to be alone. At times, I hardly knew they were there. They hadn't found jobs, though there were interviews, and all seemed to be going relatively well.

Time, however, has a way of wearing down the patience.

I became preoccupied with their messy room, which I couldn't resist peeking into at times. Dirty clothing was strewn on the floor, the bed was unmade, and there were soda cans and chip bags which often fell onto the floor from their strategic placement on their cluttered single desk. I had made it clear that I would not encroach, but this became more difficult with time. Occasionally, I'd get this itchy feeling in my spine, a need for order. It was hard for me, a neat freak, to accept their messy style. When Max didn't fulfill his laundry job and Lulu ignored the recycling, I felt a growing compulsion to act.

The day came when I entered their room on the pretext that I needed to check the fire exit door. It was located in a narrow room adjacent to theirs, which Max called his "art studio." I was unable to open the door because of large pieces of cardboard that Max had crafted into Halloween warrior costumes. I had made it very clear that this space was not to be used for storage. I imagined our charred remains should we need to escape the fire.

When Max and Lulu returned from their morning job search, I called my daughter into my room. When I reminded her of the house rules, she avoided eye contact.

"Lulu," I added, "it's a fire hazard."

"Mom," she said, now looking me in the eye. "We're going to clear it out, end of story." She lifted her eyebrows, punctuating the message with a head bob.

"It's not negotiable," I told her, holding her stare. "Do it now."

"Why don't you give her a chance?" Max yelled from outside the bedroom door. "You treat her like she's a child, and she can't stand up to you. Will you throw us out if we don't do what you say?"

I was stunned by his loud confrontation. A silence followed and I needed to act. I opened the door. "Come into the living room," I said. "We need to talk." I felt uneasy as I realized I didn't know him that well. Max had done one tour in Iraq and was discharged a year after his return. I wasn't privy to the reason.

Before I could move, Max blocked my path, his face nearly touching mine. He stood a foot taller than I, adding to my sense of being menaced. "And what if I don't?" he demanded. Did he see me as a woman he could push around? I was frightened, but determined not to show it.

I felt myself shaking. My mind shifted to high alert, and there was a quiet whizzing sound behind my eyes, one that I'd learned to trust after fifteen years of working in a psychiatric hospital.

"If you don't," I responded, my voice calm, "I'll have to call the police. Your aggressive tone makes me feel unsafe." I pulled out my cell phone, which I always carried in my bra, and began to dial. As a single parent, I was used to taking charge in a crisis, but I wondered if I'd overreacted. Lulu ran crying to the living room, and Max followed.

"I'm not a violent person," Max pushed out, his voice constricted.

"Good," I said. "Then let's talk." I closed my phone.

I took the chair across from where they were perched on the sofa.

As I spoke, my voice was firm and direct. "I will not be disrespected in my own home. Never. That's number one. And, two, Lulu *does* know how to stand up to me, and she can fight her own battles. Third, I have no immediate plans to kick you out. However, you do need to follow the house rules that we agreed to when you moved in. No exceptions." Short and sweet, it was my best shot. This was not a time for flexibility.

I wasn't prepared for what came next. Tears flooded Max's face, and then he stood up and walked over to me. Leaning down, he embraced me. "I'm sorry," he said.

I massaged his back, my *high* alert downgraded to *medium*. I'd never had a son, and I'd had a difficult relationship at times with my father and brother. What was more, I hadn't been close to a man for years, so I was moved by witnessing this young man's apparent struggle to contain his conflicted desires to be himself, but be the man I imagined his military father expected.

He returned to the sofa. By this time, Lulu had stopped crying and I no longer felt afraid. I saw their faces, contrite and gentle, and I shifted to *low* alert. "Apology accepted," I offered. "I have a temper too, and I lose it sometimes. It's okay. Let's start fresh."

"She means it, Babe." Lulu told him. "She doesn't hold a grudge." I was proud that my daughter knew my strengths. God knows she knew my weaknesses.

After a few moments of silence, they thanked me and left the room.

As I later thought about what had happened, I wondered if things might have gone differently, had I known how to talk more easily about our differences. Was I failing to grasp the cultural message of the so-called Boomerang Generation? What were the implications of two generations being pushed by financial circumstances to live together after having lived separately and independently, perhaps even having fashioned differing values and points of view? Did I need to redefine authority in order to open the conversation between us? Could I be clearer about my own needs, yet at the same time more respectful of theirs?

I had learned early in life to take care of myself. Today, I like the control it gives me. I appreciate being able to protect myself. Negotiation once seemed dangerous because it exposed the vulnerable underside of my self-protection. I now live in a world where interdependence is increasingly valued, and respecting differences is a revered way of life, especially in my diverse Berkeley community. I am made aware by the media that differences are a source of antagonism, even violence, on the national and international stage.

Though I see myself as open-minded, living with my daughter and her husband has caused me to revisit my judgments about how people ought to be. I've also noticed how hard it is to let go of these beliefs.

    I have a lot to learn.

THE WISDOM OF WAITING

It was 2013, a chilly fall afternoon, and I sat on the sofa in my cozy upstairs apartment awaiting the arrival of two inspectors hired by the potential buyers. There were two because, as the realtor explained, a second opinion is always good. I knew that there was no second opinion when it came to the Rent Stabilization Board's policy that tenants cannot be evicted simply because the house is sold, or if the house goes into foreclosure.

Slim, my on-site landlady for twenty years, had apparently been in denial that she was close to losing the house. Given her years of unconventional rent practices, I wasn't surprised. Karma catches up. She had tried to evict me five years earlier, but it was illegal so I fought it and won. Two years later she tried to force a "family move-in" eviction, saying her son Julep wanted to live in my apartment, though I knew they were estranged. Because I was a senior long-term tenant, I again prevailed. I had planned on staying for the long haul, though at times I questioned my commitment. As a single woman with limited resources, I couldn't imagine ever owning my home.

After what felt like an endless and sometimes frightening struggle against Slim's shenanigans, a judge finally approved a restraining order. That was the previous year, when Slim had escalated from writing letters falsely accusing me of peeking in her windows or rifling through her mailbox, to bellowing unspeakable things at me when I walked silently down the driveway toward my car. I came to dread the descent from my refuge in my rear upper flat, where I was surrounded by ancient pines that were home to squirrels who shot across the deck, sending my dog skidding after them.

The mar of Slim's toxic behavior had been ameliorated by the comfort of my home and by my mentors and friends at the Zen Center next door. Over the years, Slim had been an evocative real-life teacher. I had learned to let her actions roll off my back like sweat after pulling weeds in the yard. But the house sale had stirred up old feelings, despite the fact that it heralded a new beginning.

Things had quieted down, thanks to the restraining order and the surprise appearance of Julep as apartment manager. Now Julep had been forced to step in as Slim's Power of Attorney, hoping to execute a painless sale and relocate Slim and the contents of her crowded lower flat. After he had gone to the effort of clearing everything into dumpsters and moving pods, and had arranged a vacation for Slim to another state, she refused to go. To add to the problem, the house hadn't sold. And while the realtor sometimes kept me in the loop, Julep didn't talk to me except to thank me for the rent check. Unlike his mother, he was refreshingly all business.

There was finally interest in the house. The potential buyer was clever, having entered the market early, making a low offer that was refused, only to be reconsidered later when no other offers were made. I imagined that she now had the upper hand. The realtor revealed that the sale was delayed because no one wanted to buy a house with a built-in tenant, especially someone whose rent was low, but I knew that my small apartment took up less than ten percent of the overall property. It seemed to me that Slim and Julep were simply holding out for a higher price than the property was worth, hoping to drive me out. They offered to pay me to leave, but I didn't bite. A two-bedroom apartment in Berkeley with a monthly rent of under one thousand dollars was an investment I couldn't afford to forfeit, especially now that I was retired.

I heard footsteps ascending the stairs to the deck outside my apartment. The realtor knocked and I shouted for him to come in.

Introductions were made. Mari, the 50-something buyer, and her partner, Jo, both looking trim and fit, wore jeans and t-shirts. With them was one of the inspectors, Selena, a woman of around forty wearing a tweed jacket, horn-rimmed glasses and a warm smile. She apologized for the intrusion.

There were many structural issues to be considered, but everyone seemed to agree that the foundation and dry rot were the main issues.

The task was to evaluate the deck, which apparently wasn't retrofitted for earthquakes and needed to be replaced, and to consider how soon the invisible dry rot in my bathroom, revealed by the pest report, needed to be addressed. Mari's decision about making a final offer on the property, I had been told by the realtor, rested on the results of the inspection. The realtor said that Mari was probably wondering if it was worth replacing the deck and tearing up the bathroom to replace the dry rot in the walls and floor, especially since the place was inhabited by a low-paying tenant. He failed to mention that only emergency repairs had been done in the last twenty years, which was a testament to the current state. I had maintained the interior of my apartment meticulously, but that didn't seem to count.

Could it be that Slim had met her match in Mari, who appeared to know her way around the negotiating table? Mari seemed to meet every complication of the dealings with an effortless turn, like an Aikido master, sending Slim's latest crisis right back to her. And Mari didn't seem to be in a hurry. I was hopeful that she could comfortably wade through the chaos that Slim generated and buy the property at a low price. I imagined her as an honorable landlady and a good neighbor.

Selena pointed out the two major cracks in the wall, and urged Mari to walk the length of the bathroom, apparently to experience the slight downward slope. "Ah yes," she said. "Clearly a case of uneven settlement." Mari and Jo nodded with conviction, then thanked me and left with Selena. If the dry rot was mentioned, I didn't hear it.

Five minutes later, Inspector Number Two entered, dressed in chinos and a blue work shirt. Ignoring me, he spent over a half an hour examining the cracks, checking the deck's foundations, and knocking on the support boards. In the bathroom, he tapped on the walls and floor. I was not apprised of his conclusions. The plan was for Mari to receive all written reports, and then she would consider her options. If she made a proposal to the realtor, it could be a lengthy process, taking a month or more. The house had been on the market for more than four months.

The next day, I ran into one of my mentors from the Zen center. He knew Slim and her history of abuses. I told him about the inspections, then added, "I'm optimistic, but the longer I wait, the more doubtful I become. My impatience gets the best of me. What can I do?"

He was silent for a moment, looking at me through squinted eyes. "Wait as long as it takes," he said. "But like the sleeping cat, be ready to pounce when the mouse makes a move."

Another one of his Zen lessons to ponder.

It was two months before I got word that Mari had bought the house. Slim disappeared one day. Mari and Jo moved in the next day.

Weeks later, I talked to my mentor over the fence. "I can't believe how different everything is," I said. "It's like night and day. My new landlord is kind and thoughtful, and she is respectful of my privacy. I am so grateful for my new life."

"Yes," he said. "You waited." He smiled and walked away, leaving me once again to consider the wisdom of waiting, of patience, of trusting myself.

PUBLISHED WORK

A Green Bough in My Heart, Skive Magazine, Spring/Fall 2012

Warriors in Transition, Noyo River Review, Summer 2012

Pick and Pull, Looseleaf Tea, Fall 2012

Transforming, Inquiring Mind, Spring 2013

Tumbleweed, Halfway Down the Stairs, June 2013

The Green Dragon (re-titled *The Girls with the Flower Tattoos),* The Bygone Bureau, July 2013.

Intuitively Speaking, Blood and Thunder: Musings on the Art of Medicine, Fall 2013

Wild Turkeys Rising and *Gateway,* Skive Magazine, Fall 2013

Miss Pretty, Write to Woof Anthology, Grey Wolfe Publishing, Winter 2014.

Ruby's Grace and *Ruby Revisited* (previously titled *Blood Sisters),* About Place Journal, Winter 2014.

Got Your Back, Moon Magazine, May 2014.

Ellen Woods, a writer and retired county social worker, has published thirteen of the stories in *Warriors in Transiiton* in literary journals. She has received prizes at the Soul-Making Keats Literary Competition in 2011, 2012, and 2013, and at the Mendocino Coast Writers Conference in 2012. She lives in Berkeley, CA

www.ingramcontent.com/pod-product-compliance
Lightning Source LLC
Chambersburg PA
CBHW032111090426
42743CB00007B/310